ALL
HOPE
IS
FOUND

ALL HOPE IS FOUND

REDISCOVERING THE **JOY** OF EXPECTATION

SARAH JAKES ROBERTS

W PUBLISHING GROUP

AN IMPRINT OF THOMAS NELSON

ISBN 978-1-4003-3990-7 (audiobook)
ISBN 978-1-4003-3989-1 (ePub)
ISBN 978-1-4003-3987-7 (HC)

Library of Congress Control Number: 2023938171

Printed in the United States of America
23 24 25 26 27 LBC 5 4 3 2 1

*To my mother, Serita Jakes, and her
mother, Virginia Jamison.
When I feel all hope is lost, I pull from their
stories and find the faith to take another step.*

CONTENTS

INTRODUCTION

I didn't really know what I was doing when I founded the Woman Evolve movement in 2017. I desired to launch a community that authentically connected and deliberately catered to an under-represented people group. In my mind, these were women who were well versed in everything from the latest fashion, technology, entertainment, and creative trends to mom hacks, emotional wellness, skincare, and fitness goals. Their interests would vary, but we would be connected by a shared commonality—an undeniable desire to have consistent, genuine, and transformational moments with God. These encounters would be the lens that changed the way they saw their faith, themselves, and the world around them.

I didn't think finding these women would be challenging because I also dabble in many of these things. So I ambitiously, and awkwardly, launched multiple Woman Evolve touchpoints at once: social media accounts, podcast, online shopping store, on-demand video channel, conference, and tour. I didn't have a clue what I was doing, and I learned a lot of hard lessons about leadership, team building, and vision casting along the way. I had to restructure my plan repeatedly before finding some semblance of sustainability for so many initiatives.

In 2020, I began praying about the best way to serve women when we could no longer meet for conferences and tours in person. Our team began drafting weekly devotionals that contained an anchor scripture for the week with practical application for our community. These devotionals served the women well for over a year and a half before I sensed there was still something missing. I realized that I needed to be intentional about having an annual declaration that would shape not just our devotionals but all the content across our multiple touchpoints.

That sounded simple enough, but I didn't want to just pull something out of the sky. I spent the next few days considering the plight of women in this age. What are their obstacles? Dreams? Fears? Insecurities? I wanted to see life from every possible perspective before carrying the women in my heart into my sacred time with God.

My prayer was simple: "God, what word encapsulates the focus of our ministry for the year, and how can we guide the women connected to our movement in that direction?" In 2021, I began praying about the vision for 2022, and God gave me a distinct word that instantly created excitement: *revolutionary*. I immediately got goose bumps thinking of the ways the women could overthrow limiting systems and experience divine liberation.

I wanted something just as exhilarating for 2023. I prayed again and waited for the fierce word that would slingshot the women unapologetically into their destiny. God, as usual, had other plans because the word He gave me for 2023 was so subtle, delicate, and common that I was thrown for a loop. The word was *hope*.

I wanted something with a little bit more meat on its bones. (That's a country way of saying I wanted a word that would over-whelm us with so much excitement and creativity that the year would be a breeze.) I thought *hope* was too simple and straight-forward to last for the year, but when you're walking by faith, you can't afford to be disobedient. So I shrugged and figured we'd stretch out *hope* for as long as we could.

I was only an hour into my study of hope when I realized I was swimming in deep waters. Hope is easier to identify when you're feeling it than it is to express and comprehend. It has become synonymous with desire, wishing, or wanting, but it's so much more than that.

Hope is a consciousness, a promise, and a state of being.
Hope is restorative, but it can also be painful.
Hope is contagious and deeply personal.

I began to see hope as an ocean and dove in. This book holds the treasures and breakthroughs I discovered along the way.

I know I told you that I wanted God to give me a word

Hope is easier to
identify when you're
feeling it than it
is to express and
comprehend.

that had more depth than *hope* when I originally embarked on this journey. I think I felt this way because at the time it felt so straightforward and easy to understand.

Hope is one of those words that is used so casually and cavalierly that it's come to have many definitions. I can remember when "hoping this finds you well" was a fresh and kind way of starting an email before jumping into business. Now it's become so standard that it's lost its finesse. I challenge you to count how many times you say *hope* in one week. You'd be blown away at how often hope is near but far. How is it that we can use a word countless times throughout a day but still hunger for it in the deepest part of our soul?

Hope is not lost or ambiguous. It is camouflaged in the stresses, worries, and everyday hustling of our busy lives. Hope doesn't always come knocking on the door with an opportunity that brings you joy. Instead, if you want to find hope, you'll have to roll up your sleeves and open your heart to the most rewarding scavenger hunt you'll ever experience. The pursuit of hope does not disappoint.

No matter how many times hope has been lost, it can always be found.

DIVINE EXPECTATION

It's no secret that the diet culture in America is big business. When I say big business, I mean to the tune of $71 million annually.[1] That's certainly not chump change. With a little investigation, we can easily surmise that the decades-long success of the diet industry has been aided and abetted by unrealistic beauty standards for women. It takes a lot of confidence to resist seeing yourself as too big, small, flabby, broad, dark, pale, and so on. Thankfully, I'm finally coming to a place where I'm learning to fully appreciate and enjoy this body God gave me.

My thighs may never practice social distancing, my hips may always have dips, and my arms will likely always have a little extra jiggle when I wiggle, but I'm choosing to no longer cringe when I look in the mirror. I like what I see, and it's not like anything I see on TV. That's a major win! I've recently found a workout regimen I enjoy and don't see as a chore. Another win! I've also learned the beauty of moderation while discovering foods that are more nutrient-dense and delicious so eating right doesn't feel so wrong. Winner! Winner! Grilled chicken dinner!

This is still new to me, though. I unexpectedly came to this place on February 16, 2022, when I quit a health challenge I had been doing with friends. I know the exact date because I was engaged in a challenge that was supposed to last seventy-five days. Heavy emphasis on the "supposed to" because I gave up at forty-eight days. Most people in my circle were impressed I made it that long on my first attempt. Somewhere along the way, the challenge ceased being about achieving a fitness goal and became an unnecessary stressor in my life.

In addition to a few personal growth requirements, the challenge included working out twice a day (once inside and once outside) for a set amount of time, drinking a gallon of water daily, and sticking to a diet with no cheat meals or alcohol allowed. I started off strong and competitive because I wanted to see my body change. Initially, I enjoyed the mental fortitude required to push past my personal limits. I began waking up earlier and finding creative ways to work out twice a day.

I started seeing results almost instantly. If you're well versed in diet culture, as I am, you know that I wasn't losing fat but water weight. I didn't care, though, because that scale was being brought into captivity to the obedience of Christ (2 Corinthians 10:5). For thirty days, I was on a roll. I survived eating out and refused some of my favorite guilty pleasures. I'd watch my husband eat something I couldn't and roll my eyes. But it turned out the diet was not the hard part. The real challenge for me was the two-workouts-a-day requirement. Do you know how hard it is to work out twice a day when once a day is already a significant improvement from nothing?

At first, I liked the soreness after my workouts. It made me feel accomplished. But when that aching didn't dissipate, completing even the simplest task became a chore. Sitting down to use the restroom triggered PTSD from a morning filled with squats and dead lifts. My body was becoming more toned, but my negative attitude must have been lifting weights, too, because it was getting stronger and stronger.

The alarm clock went off, and I rolled my eyes at the prospect of another hard workout. Surprisingly, once I got up and moving, I was fine. The evening is when I was most likely to quit. Why would I be closer to quitting at the completion of a day as opposed to the beginning? Because I couldn't go to sleep without dreading the pain the next day promised to bring.

Expectation Is Slippery

Eventually, my expectation that more suffering was on the way forced me to relinquish my hope of successfully attaining my goal. I quit the challenge, but I learned a valuable lesson: the direction of your expectation is crucial to your quest for hope.

The direction of

your expectation

is crucial to your

quest for hope.

I'm sure you've heard someone mention a promising opportunity but then temper their enthusiasm with the phrase, "But I don't want to get my hopes up." You've probably uttered that phrase yourself. Can I be a good friend and burst your bubble? Your hopes are already up. The reason the prospect of a specific hope becoming a reality is meaningful to you is that the hope was once out of reach. A more accurate phrase would be, "I don't want to expect this to work out and increase my risk of disappointment."

It's easy to temper your excitement. You can continue qualifying your expectation a little while longer, but when you do, I just want you to know that I hear your truth. I hear you saying that you're not ready for your expectation to be fulfilled. My question to you is this: If you don't want your expectation to turn toward hope, where is your expectation currently positioned?

I quit the health challenge when I began expecting pain, fatigue, exhaustion, and frustration. But what if I had not quit? Imagine if the challenge had no end, and each day I woke up with dread because all I expected to experience during the day was difficulty. When the ups and downs of life leave us battered and bruised, expecting the worst feels like the only way to survive.

When it comes to our expectations, however, there is another option—and it's guaranteed to make you more than a survivor. You must learn to redirect your expectation from planning for demise to anticipating the divine.

Only when I began the process of unpacking hope did I

understand how slippery expectation can become over time. One of my few childhood memories with my mother's late brother, Aldo Ray, was watching him come home after fishing. He'd bring the fish into our garage and begin preparing the fish to become dinner. Sometimes he'd let us hold one of them. I can still see his face—the huge grin he always had was plastered even wider than usual as he watched our small hands trying to hold on to the slimy, erratic fish. Uncle Ray made sure he stayed close in case we became overwhelmed and needed intervention.

My young mind didn't understand what the worst-case scenario could have been had we gotten overwhelmed. The fish wasn't a vicious animal that could harm us. I assumed dropping the fish we were planning to clean and eat would not have been all that terrible. Now I know that dropping the fish was the least of Uncle Ray's concerns. He likely understood that while the fish were floundering, our bodies were too. We were beginning to mimic the fish's movement in an effort to keep it in our hands. The risk wasn't that we would drop the fish. The risk was that we'd stumble, fall, or hurt ourselves while trying to keep it within our grasp. If my uncle had to choose between the fish and us, I know he would have chosen us.

I can imagine that this is what happens when God is watching us hold on to our expectations for our lives. There are certain expectations that slip through our hands, and it hardly bothers us at all. If you're expecting chicken to be on sale at the store, but beef is on sale instead, then it's easy to pivot and adjust your plan. Then there are moments when big expectations become less and less tangible. Those are the ones that really hurt. Desperately trying to hold on to those expectations like children grasping slippery fish, we easily become frustrated, irritable, and exasperated.

Some people choose to internalize those feelings and struggle within, while others choose to release their frustrations on those who surround them. No matter where you fall on that spectrum, trying to hang on to an expectation that keeps your heart open and joy nearby can feel like being on a roller coaster.

Divine Expectations

If the fruition of what you're expecting would produce a deeper level of trust in God, wholeness for yourself, and inspiration to others, then you know it's a divine expectation. This divine expectation is a clue as to where God desires to bring healing and restoration to your life.

Now, God's vision for how that expectation will be fulfilled and your vision for how it will be fulfilled may be completely different. Time and time again in the Old Testament, God and the children of Israel shared a mutual expectation of liberation from captivity, yet they had completely different plans for how that freedom would be accomplished. Just because an expectation is divine doesn't mean it will perfectly align.

This is where a divine expectation can turn into a slippery

fish. When you manage to hold on to a divine expectation for your life, your hope doesn't feel like a faraway dream or wish; it feels like a guarantee. The stakes would be much greater if you were tasked with hanging on to a slippery fish over deep water. That hope would be much more out of reach. One wrong move and the fish would return to its home, and the probability of you falling in the water would be heightened. When a tragedy occurs in our lives, two things happen at once: the actual event and the less noticeable slipping of divine expectation from our spirit.

Divine expectations are always under attack. If the attack doesn't come from your fears and doubts, then pressure and disappointment in your environment will wage their attack. A series of unfortunate circumstances can easily convince you to let go of a divine expectation altogether.

I've heard countless stories of women who found themselves overextended, exhausted, insecure, and hurt when their attempts to hold on to their divine expectation were met with tremendous resistance. Most of the time, they leave me messages that include some variation of, "I'm trying to hang on to hope, but. . ." They then share how their lives are not moving in the direction of their hopes. I do my best to pray for and connect with as many of them as I can, but eventually I realize they aren't actually trying to hang on to hope. They're trying to hang on to the expectation that their hope is still possible.

You don't have to be a Bible scholar to have heard the popular proverb, "Hope deferred makes the heart sick" (Proverbs 13:12).

When we say we're trying to hold on to hope, we say that as if we can actually let the hope go. Even if our hopes no longer feel attainable, that doesn't mean that we forget them altogether. Instead, we bury them under difficult realities, disappointment, rejection, pressure, or stress.

I can still recall wanting to be a doctor when I was in kindergarten. I can also remember when the first shovel of dirt hit that hope. It was in a science class in high school. I knew that if I was struggling with science in high school, it was highly unlikely that I'd have the stamina to endure medical school. The expectation of difficulty buried my hope.

Divine expectation, like a writhing fish, is slippery that way. One minute you're holding on to the body, and the next you're holding on to the tail. One year we're holding on to the expectation that things are working in our favor, and the next we're holding on to the expectation that all life has to offer are challenges and disappointment. Remember my uncle who watched over me while I held the fish? God has been watching as you attempt to hold on to your expectation. Sometimes the best thing you can do is let it go and trust that God can catch you and your divine expectation.

Redirect Your Search

So far in this chapter, we've been focusing on two categories: divine expectation and expecting the worst. There's another category worth mentioning, and it's probably the most popular one because it offers an illusion of protection: expectation couch potatoes. That is in no way a judgment because we can understand how they got there. Life threw them so many curveballs that they don't know what to expect anymore. They've understandably chosen to just take life as it comes. This path offers them a certain level of protection from disappointment while leaving room for surprises.

This theory might make you protest, but hear me out: it's more dangerous to have no expectations at all than it is to have low expectations. Whether you're expecting life to be full of roses or anticipating each day will be a fight to protect your last nerve, at least you're still in the expectation game. If expectation were a muscle, then at least in either scenario you're still in the gym. Sure, your strength may be disproportionate. One arm might look like Popeye's after eating a can of spinach while the other arm looks like angel-hair pasta, but at least you've got something to work with.

The path for expectation couch potatoes is concerning because it can move you into a state of being reactive instead of proactive. Eventually the release of your creativity, wisdom, and strategy is dictated by your circumstances and not by your expectation. I know there are many of us who can relate to moments in our lives when we waited until we were down to our last before we became budget-conscious. Once we've learned that lesson a few times and have been exposed to better financial practices, we no longer spend to our limit and instead invest with our future in mind. If you're expecting disappointment, then you experience confirmation of that expectation in every situation. When someone lets you down, you say, "I knew this was going to happen." The same is true when you're expecting to be affirmed and favored. When things go well, you say, "I had a feeling this would happen!" Good or bad, what you expect, you will seek and find.

In this book, you're going to learn what chips away at your hope. You'll journey through the experiences that have crafted what you expect—or no longer expect—from yourself, God, and others. I am going to explain how to train your mind and posture your heart to expect and suspect that the goodness of God is in every circumstance.

Paul's Renewed Divine Expectation

When it comes to the awakening of renewed divine expectation, there are few stories more epic than that of the apostle Paul in Acts 9. Paul had a hope to preserve Jewish religion and customs, but he was finding it hard to hold on to his expectation that it was possible because of those pesky and persistent disciples of Jesus.

In Acts 8, Paul was on a mission to persecute anyone who was spreading the fame of Jesus throughout his region. From his perspective, Jesus was a radical heretic who was damaging the traditional Jewish faith. Though Jesus had ascended nearly four to seven years prior, His disciples were still moving with such power and authority that the only way to stop their influence was to kill them altogether. Paul traveled to Damascus fully expecting to carry out the mission of persecuting more disciples. Acts 9 details the moments when Paul's divine expectation slipped through his hands.

Paul had not even arrived in Damascus when he had an encounter with Jesus. I have to first underscore how amazing it is that Paul even had this encounter with Jesus. If you've ever flipped through a Bible that colors the words of Jesus in red, you know that the first four books of the New Testament are full of Jesus' words. After the early books of the New Testament, His words become noticeably sparser. He completed the work of the cross, was resurrected, and then ascended to heaven. He left His work in the hands of the disciples to continue carrying out into the world.

One of the reasons I love Paul's story is that it speaks to the lengths Jesus is willing to go to help us reposition our hearts, thoughts, and actions. Jesus knows how to be in many places at once. As much as He was in heaven, seated at the right hand of the Father and making intercession on our behalf, He also took the time to turn His power in Paul's direction. This truth could empower you if you struggle with feeling like you're bothering people, if you truly allow it to sink into your heart.

That gives me chills. It's so powerful that I want to make it even more personal for you. Jesus cares so much about where you have gotten off track that He will stop what He's doing in heaven to help you start over. If no one has ever told you, then let me be the first to let you know: you're worth stopping for.

Now, back to the moment when Paul was positioned to receive his divine expectation. When Jesus called to Paul from heaven, He didn't tell him everything at once. For those who don't know, Paul went on to be a big shot in the kingdom of heaven. He wrote most of the books in the New Testament, but it didn't all happen at this moment.

First, Jesus questioned Paul's actions, and then He illuminated that Paul's efforts to stop the growth of the gospel would be futile. Given his intense commitment to persecuting followers of Jesus, I can imagine this news would have been disappointing and infuriating for Paul to hear. If we were Jesus, the conversation probably would have ended there, but correction without redirection leaves people stuck. Jesus could have just left Paul in that disappointing revelation, but instead He offered him a new path. It's so comforting to me that Jesus didn't leave Paul confused, disappointed, or directionless.

Paul's belief system had been upended and his next steps were unclear, but he didn't shut down or run away. Paul stayed in the tension of disappointment and learned a valuable lesson: his disappointment would not have the final say. Because he managed to stay open, he was able to receive the next steps from Jesus. You can read the actual command in Acts 9:6, but I'd like to offer you a more personal translation. Jesus essentially told

Paul, "Keep moving in the direction you were headed but with a renewed divine expectation."

Immediately after this encounter, Paul followed Jesus' instructions, but he had to be physically led because he could no longer see. Paul was temporarily blind, but the eyes of his expectation were clearer than they'd ever been. They weren't dim from anger, the need to control, or disappointment, and they weren't stuck in a place of confusion or idleness.

Reviving Your Divine Expectation

So often when you have a devastating collision with the unexpected, it doesn't just stop you in your tracks; it shakes everything you've ever believed to be true. It strips you down and leaves you with very little to hold on to. This is the stage where many resign from being proactive and instead just wait and see what comes their way. If life has left you with little to hold on to, if you've shut down or have started indulging in unhealthy distractions to dull the pain, then I want to invite you to play the waiting game.

Go back to the place where your divine expectation was lost. You likely weren't calling it that then, but the characteristics of divine expectation include feeling favored, optimistic, seen, and understood. Divine expectation is the belief that you're not alone and somehow things are going to work out in a way that leaves you better than you were before. Going to that place after

Divine expectation is the

belief that you're not alone

and somehow things are

going to work out in a

way that leaves you better

than you were before.

disappointment can elicit an almost unbearable vulnerability. Still, stay there. Allow that divine expectation to take up space. Let it be revived.

I no longer wonder why Jesus blinded Paul on that road to Damascus. Sometimes the only way to experience the fullness of God's love for you is to close your eyes to what's happening around you and focus on what is coming alive in you.

HUNGRY FOR HOPE

1. What is the difference between having no expectations and having hope? Which route makes more room for God?
2. When was the last time you lived in expectation of something? Try to think back to that moment. What did it feel like?
3. What's something currently in your life that you can practice divine expectation with?

EXPECTATION TRANSFORMS

If we were playing *Family Feud* and Steve Harvey asked you, "What is the key to a happy marriage?" what would your answer be? Most people would say, "Communication" without taking the time to think it through. It's become an automatic response that we've picked up from hearing couples speak. Depending on what day it is and what's happening in my world, I'd probably say the same thing. But when I really take the time to ponder what I love the most about my husband and what I've noticed about the beautiful, decades-long marriages that are in my village, I believe the answer is friendship.

It's funny how that happens. I started off looking for Prince Charming, and I must admit, my husband did not disappoint. I got all the first-date goodness in my late twenties that I'd never had before. Everything else was "kicking it" that turned into a situationship. There was no chivalry involved or required. Touré, my husband, romanced me—beautiful dates, flowers, great conversation, good-morning text messages, and all the things. When we got married, he kept those things coming, but we started mixing in other things too.

The cocktail of marriage and all the things required to make it strong and sweet is another book entirely. I'll just say that we didn't know exactly what we were doing, but we knew we loved each other. We threw everything we had into our marriage. We started mixing in alternative perspectives on parenting, childhood traumas, collective visions for the future, boundaries for communication, mutually agreed-upon TV shows, and so much more. I thought we were building a marriage, and we were—but we're many years in now, and I realize that our courtship truly transformed into a beautiful friendship.

I should have known that when I asked him to grab scissors and cut out the part of my hair extensions I could not see, we'd moved beyond love and adoration and into a place that feels safer and more unshakable. It's not dependent on romantic gestures and fancy dinners. It's the beauty in doing nothing together that makes me want to experience everything with him. My heart was positioned for my husband, but God blessed me with a friend.

Remember when we took the time to discover where your divine expectation was left behind? It wasn't just so that you could make room to reintroduce hope into your life. It's because divine expectation is the building block that produces faith. Hebrews 11:1 reminds us that "faith is the substance of things hoped for, the evidence of things not seen." Expectation produces faith, and faith insists that the abnormal become normal.

We are not shaking up your life with renewed expectation and the epic pursuit of hope only for you to go back to your norm. We're getting you out of your comfort zone and into your go zone—the space where the abnormal eventually becomes your new normal because you refused to give up.

Defying Expectations

I've been the first one to admit that, growing up, my connection with faith felt tattered and torn. It's ironic because my upbringing as a pastor's kid was surrounded by the miraculous and undeniable presence of God, but I had very few personal encounters. Most of those moments I shrugged off as isolated occurrences and did not lean into the opportunity to take those moments and turn them into a rich spiritual life.

When I found out I was pregnant a few months shy of my fourteenth birthday, I figured any shot I had at tapping into faith was, well, shot. One thing I knew, though, was that I would not allow the added responsibility of being a teenage mother to keep me from establishing a safe and stable life for my son.

Everyone made sure that I realized how hard motherhood was going to be and how unlikely it would be for me to keep up academically and professionally with other girls my age. I started

Expectation produces

faith, and faith insists

that the abnormal

become normal.

busting my tail to defy their expectations. I graduated from high school early and entered college, because my mission was to defy the expectations of my circumstance. Eventually, I burned out, and my college grades started suffering. I dropped out, and my life started spiraling downward. What happened from there is a long story that I detail in my memoir, *Lost and Found.*[2]

I'm sharing this story now because it speaks to how the desire to defy expectations is rooted in a belief system that has elements of faith. While I was unsure how to have consistent faith in God, one thing that is pervasive in our culture is how to have faith in ourselves. This motivation is often enough to get the ball rolling in the direction of purpose, but it is not sustainable. Have you ever met a woman who is counting only on herself? I already know somebody is like, "Yes, girl! I am she!" Sometimes she feels on top of the world; other days she feels like she's being buried under it.

Having faith in ourselves feels admirable, but it can also be a trauma response when we don't feel like anyone else has faith in us or when we don't have faith in the people around us. Clinging to faith in ourselves is often the last resort before sinking into an abyss of loneliness and despair.

A part of my restoration has involved coming to a place where I see my existence as a reflection of God's faith in my ability to navigate the life that He's given me. It's been humbling and empowering to live with the perspective that I am alive because God values my unique identity and believes it adds value to His kingdom.

There's a man in the Bible named Job, and his book of the Bible begins with a dialogue between God and Satan. Satan was walking the earth looking for someone to torment. God volunteered Job to withstand the plans of the Enemy because God had faith in Job's ability to withstand the testing and trials without allowing those tests and trials to make him turn his back on God.

I won't be campaigning for God to volunteer me for any additional tests and trials anytime soon, but I do use the knowledge that God believes in our ability to preserve our faith even when life is heartbreaking as a sign of His faith in us. I used to think of myself as random and inconsequential, but then I realized there's not one thing God has created that does not serve a purpose. Mosquitoes, gnats, and flies, as annoying as they are, serve the larger ecosystem. Alligators, lions, and bears can be scary and vicious, yet they, too, serve a purpose. Why would God get to me and make my life and everything in it random? I firmly believe that everything in my life is serving me in becoming who God believes I can be. If it doesn't serve a purpose or it's serving as a distraction, the moment I realize it's a distraction, there's subtraction.

We see evidence of God's faith in His creation to reign over their responsibilities in Genesis 1:28–31:

> Then God blessed them, and God said to them, "Be fruitful and multiply; fill the earth and subdue it; have dominion over the fish of the sea, over the birds of the air, and over every

living thing that moves on the earth." And God said, "See, I have given you every herb that yields seed which is on the face of all the earth, and every tree whose fruit yields seed; to you it shall be for food. Also, to every beast of the earth, to every bird of the air, and to everything that creeps on the earth, in which there is life, I have given every green herb for food"; and it was so. Then God saw everything that He had made, and indeed it was very good.

The faith God has in us to be fruitful, multiply, fill the earth, subdue it, and have dominion has not changed, but it is now riddled with more complications than necessary. It's not because God changed His mind about having faith in us, but rather that we lost faith in God. Still, God is gracious to offer us a path back to that intention through Jesus. My relationship with Jesus is rooted in my belief that the path to the highest version of myself will be manifested through modeling my life after Him.

You know what's crazy about that? I still have faith in myself, but the faith I have is in the me I've become through trusting God. I have faith in who I'm becoming by walking out my life with Jesus.

Every morning is a reminder that God still has faith in our ability to access His power to bring heaven to earth, that Jesus overcame the obstacles that make it feel impossible, and that the Holy Spirit is with us to comfort us in dark times and collaborate with us in hard times. We never have to feel completely alone.

From the outside looking in, it may appear that it's just me—but, girl, I'm working with a winning team.

Every now and then, I still have moments when I fall back into that "I've only got myself" mentality. Yes, even with my husband, children, family, team, and ministry. I start to get nervous about whether I've got what it takes, and when a few disappointments occur, I'm back to questioning myself and reliving the many memories of failure from my past. That's when I know that my faith needs a pivot. I spent a decade after my teen pregnancy living to prove other people wrong until I realized that what I really needed to do was to pivot my faith toward living out God's faith in me.

Powered by If

I love speaking to all groups, but I admit something special takes place when I'm fortunate to share space with women. I have enjoyed catering to the unique needs of modern womanhood by understanding the similarities of women in Scripture who received God's transformational identity for their lives. One of the women in the New Testament I've been able to identify with the most is a woman whose name we don't know but whose circumstance allows many of us to relate. Scripture tells us this woman had an issue of blood for twelve years. Our good sister's Aunt Flo came to visit and didn't go home.

According to the customs of this time, the woman was not just inconvenienced by this flow, but she was also isolated. At that time, a menstruating woman was supposed to stay home and be untouched until her flow ended. Can you imagine going into seclusion one day thinking your period would last only a few days, and it turned into twelve years? The initial worry would yield to concern, then concern would become a mixture of grief, anger, loneliness, and fear.

I know that many of us can relate to this woman. Issues we were sure would last only a short time in our lives have haunted us for years. Like the woman in Scripture, our wounds have also created isolation, fear, anger, and frustration. At some point, she probably felt like giving up on the pursuit of healing. Maybe there were weeks when she allowed the depression to win a few rounds. Maybe you did, too, but if you're reading this book, then you've decided to start swinging again.

Luke 8 informs us that the woman had spent all her livelihood on physicians, trying to receive a cure, but nothing worked. I won't even get into all the physicians I've met along the way in my attempts to address the issues of low self-esteem, abandonment, and rejection that were flowing through my soul. Suffice it to say that some of the "physicians" I sought looked like achievement, toxic friendships, codependency, weed, and alcohol. Our physicians come in many different shapes and sizes, but none of them leave us cured in the way that we desire.

This woman with the issue of blood won my admiration

because she was determined to defy the expectations of her issues. She didn't just sit back and allow her condition to have the final say. She should have given up, but she kept her heart open for a revolution of her issues. If you can in any way relate to this woman, your fight to survive and defy the expectations of your issues is your superpower.

There comes a moment, though, when your superpower needs backup. It's the moment when you realize that you can no longer go at it alone. Because defying the expectations of your circumstances is only sustainable if your objective is to meet the expectations of what God says is possible for your life. That's something heaven can get behind. When the woman in Luke 8 needed some backup, she aligned herself to defy the expectations of her issues and positioned herself to receive the healing that God desires for us all.

The gospels of Matthew, Mark, and Luke all share the story of this woman, and each of them offers us a different detail that gives us greater insight into what she was thinking. Matthew 9:21 tells us that the woman said to herself, "If only I may touch His garment, I shall be made well."

She had an expectation of what Jesus could do that would take her from trying to defy expectations and welcome her into a space of healing, rest, connection, breakthrough, and freedom. Often, when I have heard this text preached, the woman's determination is highlighted. But Matthew let us know that while she was determined, she wasn't sure she could actually achieve her goal, saying, *"If only . . ."*

When you procrastinate about moving in the direction of healing because you aren't sure whether healing can happen, you've missed the opportunity to be powered by "if." What would you do differently if you allowed yourself to be powered by "if"? *If* I am anointed? *If* I can be healed? *If* I can recover? *If* I can write? *If* I can inspire? *If* I can develop?

This heroic woman in the Bible did not let her "if" pass her by, and neither should you.

From Expectation to Faith

Let's consider the posture of the woman with the issue of blood before she began pressing through the multitudes to touch the hem of Jesus' garment:

Sis was tired.
Sis was determined.
Sis was in need.
Sis was defiant.
Sis was unsure.
Sis was my kind of girl.

Can you imagine the nerves and the pressure she was under in that moment? She needed to move in and move out through the crowd without anyone really seeing her, but she needed to be close enough to the Man who could heal her that healing was within reach. This was a top-priority mission with high stakes, and call me dramatic, but I can't help but see the woman as some version of an Angelina Jolie character in the early 2000s.

The woman eventually made her way to Jesus. She grabbed the hem of His garment, and immediately the flow of blood stopped. She felt it in her body without even having to check for the evidence. There's nothing like the moment when you *know* you're no longer the same.

The story should have ended there. She got her healing; Jesus was on the move. There was no need for Jesus to stop and acknowledge her, but this is the most powerful portion of the text. While most people focus on the woman's tenacity to touch Jesus, I'm mesmerized by Jesus' desire to go out of His way to touch her.

Jesus was surrounded by a crowd, but He asked, "Who touched Me?" (Luke 8:45). The disciples were confused. Jesus was essentially in a mosh pit asking who touched Him. But He realized that while other people were just brushing and bumping against Him, someone had actually touched Him with her need, not her desire to be connected to His clout.

The woman came out of the crowd, fell before Him, and spilled all the tea about her issues, her reasoning, and her healing. I don't know if she worried that He'd reprimand her for breaking the rules of the custom, but what He did next, I'm sure she did not anticipate. Jesus claimed her as His daughter.

Jesus said to this woman, "Daughter, be of good cheer; your faith has made you well" (v. 48). The woman who'd been isolated and untouchable was coronated and crowned. She would have settled for the issue to stop flowing, but Jesus did so much better than that.

Isn't it crazy how God has a plan for our lives that is beyond what we're willing to settle for? This is truly divine hope. I know what it's like to be a woman with issues that won't stop flowing. When I finally had a genuine encounter with Jesus, I was glad to finally stop the flow of my shame and insecurity. That's all I wanted. I didn't want to feel like damaged goods anymore, but God predestined for the flow to stop *and* for me to experience the restoration of His original intention.

Notice that Jesus also told the woman to "be of good cheer." No longer would she live in fear, isolation, worry, or grief, but she would have joy again. If Jesus had not given her this permission, she could have been healed physically, but emotionally and spiritually she would still be functioning under the rules and guidelines that her issues created. Jesus broke her out of that by telling her it was okay for her to have good cheer.

This is a word for someone holding this book. Perhaps it's even a preview of what's to come for you. You desire healing and breakthrough from your issues, but are you also prepared to be restored as if your issues had never happened in the first place? Can you do the work of releasing the identity your issues created and experience the identity that comes with healing?

That woman is not an island.

That woman has joy.

That woman is healed.

That woman is you.

My favorite part of this text is when Jesus told the woman, "Your faith has made you well." It wasn't her touching Him that made her well. It was her faith. I love this because nowhere is it mentioned that the woman had faith. All the woman possessed was an expectation that if she could touch Jesus, she would be healed. Jesus told the woman she would not have been able to expect an outcome of healing unless there was a deposit of faith fueling her. Her faith gave her permission to expect the impossible. So does yours! Your faith is on assignment to change your expectation.

Being told to "just keep the faith" while your issues whup your behind makes you want to fight the person speaking the words. Chile, how can you keep the faith when you don't even trust what to have faith for? I hang on to my faith by remembering that I see only half the picture. I trust that if I work what I can see, then God will take care of the rest. Sometimes that work is just keeping my heart pure.

When you don't know where or how to keep your faith, protect your expectation. Expect the divine intervention of God to make the difference. Listen for the moments when you hear that God is working, and then move in the direction of where God is moving. You may have to seek out those testimonies if they aren't

Your faith is on

assignment to

change your

expectation.

within your community. Google things like "joy after divorce," "purpose in grief," and "peace with a disease." Shift your expectation in the direction of hope, and you'll discover that your expectation transforms into faith.

HUNGRY FOR HOPE

1. Revisit the retelling of the woman with the issue of blood (Luke 8:43–48). How would you describe this woman? What did Jesus say about her faith? What obstacles did she face, and how did she choose to handle them?

2. Do you *wonder* if God will show up, or do you *expect* that He will? How might you go about turning your heart toward *hope* and *expectation* today?

3. How does relying on God take the pressure off you? How can you strengthen your faith today by placing your trust in Him?

THREE
MISPLACED FAITH

I am often asked the same question by women who are multi-tasking the many responsibilities in their lives: "How do you balance it all?" I usually quip about how I'm drowning in my sea of responsibilities just like they are. It sounds like I'm joking, and most of the time I am because I've honestly given up on the idea of balance as we desire it. My definition of *balance* is everyone in my family and on my team feeling perfectly attended to and well-adjusted to the rhythm of our demanding lives at all times. Additionally, things would also be balanced if I felt well attended to physically, spiritually, and mentally, and perfectly adjusted to the always-changing rhythm of my life. I'd also like to have financial, emotional, and creative abundance . . . at all times.

When I begin to define *balance* in this way, I soon realize that my expectations are unrealistic. So I've given up on that and have settled into a much more attainable definition of *balance*.

I attribute the freedom to experience this form of balance to my husband, who elaborates on the definition in his book of the same name.[3] If I may paraphrase, Touré shares that balance is not a formula for mastering my responsibilities; it's a commitment to being fully present as the highest version of myself in any given moment. This definition has aided me in recalibrating my consciousness of what it means to balance it all.

With this in mind, I'm better able to serve my environment. If I haven't seen the highest version of myself in days, weeks, or months, then I need to check in with the Lord and perhaps my therapist, and maybe also grab a pint of ice cream, some french fries, and/or the closest hotel where I can recenter. Once I've found myself, I can serve my community with wisdom, discernment, patience, and strategy. The freedom from performance and pressure has helped me in every area of my life, but it has had the most impact on my relationship with my children. I'm no longer performing as the societal definition of a good mother. I'm inviting my children to experience my expression of goodness as a woman with them as my audience.

My highest self wrote that last sentence. There are moments when I'm at the mercy of my children's expectations about what I should do and how I should respond. It happens most often with our youngest daughter, Ella. I don't know if there is a pressure cooker more effective than my seven-year-old. She wants what she wants when she wants it. She knows how to communicate that need and dismantle any counterargument preventing that need from being met. I'm using the word *need* very lightly here, unless you define more screen time, fruit snacks, a later bedtime, and punishment of an older sibling as a "need."

I know every parent thinks their child is Albert Einstein reincarnate, but I promise you, Ella is so smart that I need to go to law school to contend with her. We frequently travel for business and ministry. Before Ella started school, she'd travel with us. When she started school, the pandemic hit, and she was home with us 24/7. As the world began to open up again, Touré and I put her in a more traditional school environment. We drop off our two youngest daughters at school and pick them up from school when we're in town. Still, we underestimated how the increase in our collective schedules would affect our connection time as a family.

Touré and I are fortunate that we can create our own schedules, which has allowed us to drive together to take our children to school most mornings and pick them up most afternoons. We could swap and take turns, but part of the reason we double-team is that we want to get as much time with our children as possible because we know there's a likelihood that there will always be an upcoming trip. The older children have settled into our rhythm and recognize that, though we may travel more than their friends' parents, we are also able to be more present when we are home because we can build our own schedules. Ella hasn't quite caught on to that level of reasoning, but we still thought that the more quality and quantity of time we spent with her, the more likely she'd be to compromise when we needed to take a quick trip for work.

Ella didn't fall for it. It didn't matter whether we'd be back in a few months or a few days. She wanted us home. I am honored to serve as her emotional security and stability. I also value the opportunity to model for her what it looks like when a woman is walking in her purpose. Even though my role as her primary sense of emotional and spiritual security and ultimate cuddle buddy is my favorite gig, I love offering my gifts to God to serve what He's doing on the earth.

A friend shared with me a tool that helped to ease her children's disappointment when her traveling is unavoidable. (Maybe this will help other working mamas whose real CEOs are the little people who call them Mom.) My friend said she was able to make the time away less miserable for her children by planning something for them to look forward to upon her return, like making cupcakes, going to the park, or catching a film. When I first adopted this method, it barely passed the sniff test with Ella, but I took what I could get.

One day before walking out the door, I had an idea. I ran to my closet and wrapped up Ella in my big, fluffy everyday robe and asked her to cuddle with it and keep it warm while I was away. She felt honored that I would trust her with my things, and it also helped her to have a piece of me with her while I was gone. It turns out that Ella is more reasonable when I travel when she has faith for what's to come and a piece of me to hang on to until I return.

Faith After Devastation

As much as I want to tell you that possessing faith will always lead to a divine hope and shield you from any disappointment, I think we've become better friends than that, and I feel obliged to keep it one hundred with you. There have been countless times when I've heard someone say, "All you need is faith." For someone who has a healthy perspective on faith, this is true, but there are moments when our lens of faith is smudged by doubt and disappointment.

If your faith is going to serve you in every season, it can't just be robust; it also must be flexible. The goal is not to allow the faith we have for something to take away from who we have faith in.

I may not have had a personal encounter with God in my youth, but I did have personal encounters with church folks. One thing I can hear them saying in my head is, "Any way You bless me, Lord, I'll be satisfied." I don't know if there is a more relevant saying that surmises faith in God versus faith in something than this. The statement usually came after a specific request and was meant to remind God, and maybe themselves, that more than what they were praying for, they had faith in the God to whom they were praying.

If we go back to the parenting hack that I use for Ella, we see that the activity she's looking forward to is what she has faith in, but she's able to hang on to that future possibility because the presence of the robe serves as a daily reminder that I'm good for it.

The goal is not to

allow the faith we

have for something

to take away from

who we have faith in.

Over time, we've experienced countless modifications to our "welcome home" activity. The store didn't have icing for the cupcakes. My flight was delayed. A birthday party came up, or I needed to rest before putting on my mom hat. The first time Ella experienced that, she was worried that our special time together would be canceled, but the more consistent I was in making up for the setback, the more she trusted me when the next unexpected thing arose.

If I can maintain Ella's ability to have faith in what I say, then she'll trust me when I pivot from what she had faith for. She'll believe that I can make it up to her.

This is where our disconnect with God can occur. When we have faith in something that God doesn't deliver, we can lose faith in God. When our faith in God has been shot, we no longer believe that He has a plan we can trust. The goal is to get to a place of unshakable faith in God even when what we have faith in is not manifested. From this place of faith, we can say, "God, even though You didn't show up in the way that I anticipated, I trust it's because when You do show up, You're going to take into account this present grief."

It helps me to keep in mind the moments when I survived previous disappointments. I know it feels like that thing almost wiped you out completely, but this moment is evidence that it did not win. I believe God preserved you, and in time you'll see that God also preserved your faith in the midst of it all.

When is the last time you checked to make sure you didn't

have more faith in a thing than you did in God? It takes a lot of courage to admit that the failure to obtain that thing can also make you lose faith in God. I've been there, and I'm glad to report that it's possible for your faith in God to be restored. It doesn't happen because God gives you a different thing instead. It happens when you realize that even if God did nothing at all, He's been more than merciful already.

Whenever I'm believing in God for something big, I take a moment and ask myself, *If this doesn't happen, how will I feel?* I allow myself to feel the genuine disappointment and to grieve the potential of it not turning in my favor. Then I remind myself that my relationship with God is not predicated on performance— mine or His. It's difficult to pinpoint the moment because it happens so subtly. We start off praying to God that we can conceive, buy a home, get into school, scale a business, write a book, or find a partner. I may not have named your thing, but you know what your thing is.

Our prayers in the early stage sound something like this: "God, I know You're able to release Your power and bring this thing that my heart desires into my life." Then after some time, our prayers start to sound more like we're begging than believing: "God, please, if You would just bring this thing into my life, then I won't need anything else from You at all." Eventually, we run out of faith that God even hears our pleas, so we stop praying altogether. And just like that, our faith in God has been misplaced by our faith in our thing.

If you've ever hoped for something that God didn't do, you know all too well how challenging it can be to maintain your faith in God when you've had to relinquish your faith in something you were looking forward to experiencing. This is where many of us begin to ease the pain of disappointment by no longer putting our faith in things at all.

Some people are tormented because they felt that fulfillment and joy could only be experienced through one particular path. They had faith in it and even put in the work required to prepare the way for that goal to become a reality. But over time, it became clear that what they had faith in wasn't going to happen.

The parent wasn't going to get any more time to live.

The marriage was deteriorating.

The child wasn't going to experience that change in heart.

Those moments can make us feel that God disappointed us. But what I've come to learn about God is that when the thing we have faith in is not realized in the way we desire, it's because God has a perspective that requires a different path. Notice I used the word *different* and not *better*. I know there are moments when our declarations that things are working out for the best can be abrasive to people who are still nursing the tender wounds of disappointment.

Though it's well-intentioned, when we say things like "I guess God had a better plan" to someone who is grappling with the sting of grief, the devastation of disease, or the despair of abuse, the idea that God planned and approved the plan is insensitive and often untrue. I can imagine us saying, "Trust God's plan," and God nudging Jesus in heaven like, "But I ain't have nothing to do with that." (My God says *ain't* when the moment calls for it.)

Leave Room for Good

There's a verse that brings me comfort when my world is going haywire. If you've ever listened to at least six sermons or binge-watched *Manifest* on Netflix, you know it. It's Romans 8:28, and it says, "And we know that all things work together for good to those who love God, to those who are the called according to His purpose."

You know what that verse does not say? It doesn't say "all things *are* good," and it doesn't say "all things *feel* good." We do a disservice to ourselves and God when we attempt to force our pain, or anyone else's, to fit into a belief system that the terrible, dark devastation that happens in life is somehow a part of God's plan. No, trauma's headquarters is in hell. When it sends a package of destruction with your name on it, it has an intention.

We think the purpose of trauma is to take us out, but that's not true. The intention of trauma is to wipe out our faith. If you no longer have faith in anything or faith in anyone, you are rendered powerless and ineffective at establishing new healthy norms and breaking generational curses. You know why? Because you have no reason to partner with God. If you're not pointing your faith toward your destiny, then you're relinquishing the power you possess to align with the infinite ways God can meet or exceed your expectations.

One of my favorite scriptures is Isaiah 54:17: "'No weapon formed against you shall prosper, and every tongue which rises against you in judgment you shall condemn. This is the heritage of the servants of the LORD, and their righteousness is from Me,' says the LORD." Sometimes I recite this verse as a reminder to myself when the weapons that have been formed against me feel like they're prospering. It's a recitation rooted in defiance.

Then there are moments when I remind myself that there is a caveat to this promise, which is that it is preserved for a specific group: "the servants of the LORD." A servant is "one that performs duties about the person or home of a master or personal employer."[4] Some of us missed the moment when fear started signing our paychecks, but we can see it in our actions. We begin serving our disappointments with stagnancy, skepticism, and bitterness. In those moments, we are no longer living in the covering of this promise. Am I telling you to clock in and act like serving God is easy? Girl, no. All I'm saying is, God is the only employer where you can clock in, roll your eyes, do the bare minimum, and be sent to Jesus instead of the unemployment line.

Assuming a hopeful heart posture that communicates your desire to serve God through the tension is to say, "God, I'm placing my faith in Your plan even though I can see and hear my inner despair desiring to rule over me."

You may be wondering, *How can I continue to call on God when it feels like God didn't answer in the area where I needed Him the most?* It's not that God doesn't care or didn't hear. God is convinced in His ability to make the most heartbreaking equation total out to good.

From Heartbreak to Faith

I am reminded of the story of Naomi in the book of Ruth. Naomi knew heartbreak so well that she changed her name. She requested to be called Mara, a Hebrew word that means "bitter," because the loss of her husband and two sons made her feel that the Lord had dealt with her bitterly (Ruth 1:20).

If you've ever felt like you must be on God's bad side, you and Naomi would have been besties. Over the course of her story, we see how God sent her reminders that He wasn't finished dealing with her. I'm a fan of speaking the truth about where you are. Naomi obviously didn't hold back, and I believe that's why she was able to move forward even when it hurt. She didn't try to bury her frustration and rejection to make other people uncomfortable, but she also found a way to keep the eyes of her expectation open.

In the book of Ruth, we see Naomi's journey with her daughter-in-law Ruth as God revealed that He wasn't finished yet. Ultimately, Naomi found restoration, but it was not in her husband or son

I'm a firm believer

that God collects

every tear, and in

time you will witness

your miseries give

birth to victory.

coming back to life. Her restoration came in finding the goodness of God with the remainder of her life. There are some things and people God will bring back into your life, and it will be precisely what you thought was lost. Then there are things and people you'll never see again, but you will see His goodness again.

I'm a firm believer that God collects every tear, and in time you will witness your miseries give birth to victory. Then there are other things we won't fully understand on this side of heaven. I can't offer you a pretty little bow that will tie all of your things together, but prayerfully I can persuade you to take the faith you had for that thing and place it back in the jar of faith you have in God. Learn to whisper the prayer that a church mother once yelled: "Any way You bless me, Lord, I'll be satisfied."

Remember when I told you that you've got to learn to keep your faith flexible? It's because I want you to have an alternative that is more beneficial than leaving your faith in the place of your disappointment. I want you to remember the confidence you possess. It fills you with determination, power, and focus. Imagine picking it up from where it was lost and stretching it to where you are now. Your faith is not stiff. Your faith has proven it's not unmovable. So why not dare to replace your faith in your present and ask God, "Where do we go from here?"

HUNGRY FOR HOPE

1. Have you ever found yourself bargaining with God, saying, "God, if You will do just *this one thing* for me, then I'll be content"? What was the end result of that sort of prayer? Was your faith in God or in the "one thing" you asked Him for?

2. What does the definition of balance look like in your life? How can you recalibrate that to better serve your environment?

3. When is the last time you checked to make sure you didn't have more faith in a thing than you did in God?

FOUR
PREPARE FOR HOPE

If you ask any mother of a newborn child how she's doing around week eight of her baby's life, and that mother doesn't have a robust support system, then you'll see the answer in her eyes before the words even hit her mouth. The girl is stressed. She's not sure if she'll ever sleep again. She may not let you get too close just in case you pick up on the fact that she had to choose between showering and napping—and sleep won.

Theoretically, she knows that the baby she's holding in her arms will one day outgrow her constant embrace and likely sleep more hours than they're awake during their teenage years, but when you're reduced to surviving hour by hour, thinking of the future is a luxury.

In Jeremiah 29:10–14, God made a promise to His people about the future:

For thus says the LORD: After seventy years are completed at Babylon, I will visit you and perform My good word toward you, and cause you to return to this place. For I know the thoughts that I think toward you, says the LORD, thoughts of peace and not of evil, to give you a future and a hope. Then you will call upon Me and go and pray to Me, and I will listen to you. And you will seek Me and find Me, when you search for Me with all your heart. I will be found by you, says the LORD, and I will bring you back from your captivity.

God promised His people through this scripture that although they would suffer in Babylon for seventy years and their focus would be reduced to their daily survival, His plan saw beyond oppression, and in time He would make sure they could see it the way He did. Essentially, this scripture is like the fluffy robe I left with Ella to help keep her somewhat sane during my trip.

Who doesn't want to be reminded that God sees us beyond our present moment and is not out here letting the world stress us out and win? As a stand-alone verse, Jeremiah 29:11 brings peace to my soul, but in context, it illuminates the reality that in life we're guaranteed to go through some hard times. I can't help but wonder if this scripture would be as popular if it were shared in the context that it was written. Remember, this powerful promise was given in the context of catastrophic oppression.

Can we take a moment and be honest? If I have seventy hours

of stress, conflict, and complications in my life, I start praying with a little bit of side-eye, like, "Lord, are we still good?" I might be exaggerating with the seventy hours, but I still can't imagine being on the other end of this promise. God let Israel know in advance that for seventy years—*seventy years!*—they were going to be in captivity. Now, to be fair, the Israelites got themselves into this predicament by their own disobedience. God did not absolve them from the consequences of their actions, but in true God fashion, He didn't leave His people in the place they earned. He let them know that even their captivity would lead back to His goodness.

I've never experienced the type of physical oppression that Israel experienced during this time. Nor have I experienced the type of enslaved oppression that my ancestors experienced centuries ago. However, I am very familiar with the oppression of shame, doubt, fear, insecurity, and depression. When trauma becomes common, the oppression connected to it is normalized.

When those chains begin to break from your mentality, actions, and spirit, it's a sign that God is giving you His future and His hope. If you're ready for those chains to begin breaking, you have to be willing to ask yourself, *How does my perspective on this differ from how God is seeing it?* We're fortunate to see throughout Scripture how God's perspective differed from humanity's. We see that God has constantly held the highest thoughts toward His creation. It's possible for us to stretch ourselves to do the same.

For Israel, the Lord's words in Jeremiah 29:11 held significance because when you're in the process of being restricted, it's very easy to lose sight of your future. Eventually, you acquiesce to thinking every day will be the same and there is no possibility for an existence outside of the one you're presently attempting to survive.

I've spent a lot of time talking about expectation and faith in this book so far. I found this necessary because if we're going to find hope, we need to have the ingredients. I'm again reminded of Hebrews 11:1: "Faith is the substance of things hoped for." Without faith, our hope cannot become a reality. I hope that you feel your faith being restored and refilled, because I want you to start learning more about how you can use your increased faith as the primary ingredient to get you closer to experiencing hope.

Layers of Hope

In 2002, a low-budget romantic comedy took the world by storm. Written by and starring Nia Vardalos, *My Big Fat Greek Wedding* is the hilarious story of a Greek woman who falls in love with a non-Greek man and has to convince her family to accept him. The movie is filled with the kind of relatable yet unique drama that anyone who has ever embarked on the journey of joining two different families and cultures experiences.

One of the characters in the film elicits recurring amusement from viewers due to his loyalty to using Windex for any and every physical ailment. It was so random and he was so committed to this remedy that it brought to mind the way people in my personal village held a strong belief that ginger ale, saltine crackers, and a nap could fix *anything*. Fever? Lie down. Stomachache? Saltine crackers. Migraine? Ginger ale or 7UP, if you're in a pinch. All the symptoms at once? All the remedies at once, and then add some Vicks VapoRub on your feet with warm socks for extra credit.

I'm praying that something similar happens to you when you're finished with this book as it relates to hope. If I complete this divine assignment, you'll never see hope the same again. You'll understand the multifunctional application of hope in every season, and you will never feel hopeless for long again. It's because hope is both a distant desire for the future and an immediate wish for the present. Hope is a perspective for how we view what's occurring in our lives but also a state we experience when an expectation is met or exceeded. Hope can come in the form of an experience, but it can also be found in the recollections of our past. Hope is mysterious and obscure but also familiar and straightforward.

No wonder hope is fleeting. It's always on the move.

I can't help but want to tap into my grandmother's voice and say, "Hope! Get somewhere and sit down!" The realization that hope is always on the move can be frustrating. One minute it can feel like hope is everywhere, and quite literally with one call or text the next minute it feels like you'll never experience hope again. I've learned to find the beauty in the constant motion of

No wonder

hope is fleeting.

It's always on

the move.

hope. If hope were stationary, then once it's achieved, there would be nothing left to bring us excitement, highlight our insecurities, and expand our faith.

When we were children, the fulfillment of our hope elicited the same level of excitement regardless of how big or small our hopes might have been. Ella is just as excited on her birthday when she gets gifts as she is when she gets an unexpected trip to McDonald's for french fries. She is thrilled to stay up five extra minutes in the same way she's thrilled to have a weekend getaway with her grandparents. Only when we become older does the fulfillment of small hopes feel inconsequential in comparison to a big hope that seems to be stuck in the queue.

Imagine bringing the same level of joy and gratitude to arriving at work on time after a crazy morning to getting approved for the home sale after enduring multiple rejections. The problem with hope being overused is not that it becomes common; it's that the victories become common too. In time, we fail to truly acknowledge and savor how often our hopes become a reality.

Origin of Your Hope

I'm betting that when most of you picked up this book, you did so with a specific hope in mind. Or maybe you wanted to better understand how you could live in a perpetual state of hope and optimism among the many stresses of your life. These are legitimate desires. Who can't relate to the desire to maintain a hopeful perspective or the need for an extra boost of hope geared toward an outcome you think will add value to your life? Have you ever taken the time to dissect how the actualization of hope would change your life? How would it differ from what you're currently experiencing? More importantly, do you understand the origin of your hope? Where did the desire spring from in the first place, and can you trust that the hope is healthy?

I'll use my life as an example to break this concept down. Once I became a teenage mother, I had one primary hope that I really never shared with anyone, and that was for me to get married. I want to be noble and say that it was so my son could have two parents, but that would not be completely true. I wanted to get married so that I no longer had evidence that I wasn't a "good" girl.

When I was growing up, I was taught that the dominant path to virtue and worthiness could be achieved only by maintaining your virginity. I figured the next best thing was to get married as soon as possible so I would at least look like I'd done the right thing.

Currently, I'm optimistic about the transition I see taking place in Christian communities of faith that seek to acknowledge a woman's inherent worth and value outside of her virginal status. I'm going to get deep with you for a minute. If a young woman is in your sphere of influence, you have an opportunity to esteem her beyond her body. Of course, it's important that a

Any hope that

is rooted in fear

is incapable of

producing true

contentment.

young girl learns to nurture, preserve, and protect her body, but not exclusively for the sake of marriage. Her preservation should be rooted in the knowledge she has of her entire being: mind, body, soul, and spirit.

I've had many conversations with those of us who didn't keep it locked until we got that rock on our finger that we assumed all of our value was lost. I desire to see a world where we no longer reduce women to thinking they're only as valuable as the number of people they have or have not been with. When we begin to applaud the intelligent and powerful offering of a woman outside of her body, we empower her to make healthier choices in regard to her relationships and identity.

The issue with the way of thinking that I was taught is that the origin of my hope was rooted in my fear of rejection. Any hope that is rooted in fear is incapable of producing true contentment. Exploring the origin of our hope is instrumental in us determining whether that hope will actually satisfy our souls.

If you're going to explore the origin of your hope, you have to ask yourself, *Why am I hoping for this?* The more honest you can be about your why, the better. You may find that when you begin to ask this question, your reason seems trivial. If you're super critical of yourself, you may even feel like your why is immature. Now is not the time to judge yourself. Your reason is your reason, and we'll let God determine the best way to get you to His truth. It's impossible to judge yourself harshly and love yourself fully at the same time.

If your hope, like mine, is rooted in fear of any sort, then your hope can only be qualified by injecting faith, not accomplishment, into that space. The more accepting you become of the jagged edges of your story, the less you need your future to be the remedy for your past. Hope does not reverse trauma; it aids in the reconciliation of what's left. True power is when your hope and your trauma can live in the same place without one canceling the other out.

I can give you countless examples of hope and trauma living in the same place, but I don't think there is one that offers as much insight into the character of God as the moment when we find Jesus on the cross.

Qualifying Hope

One of the things that I enjoy about preaching is not just consuming and then sharing accounts of God's faithfulness throughout the generations but also realizing how the human experience has not drastically changed. Fear, doubt, insecurity, pride, love, forgiveness, compassion, hope, and all the things that make life a beautiful mosaic are laid out for us in Scripture.

The less I understood about life and the varied stages of the human condition, the more boring the Bible was. When I realized that though the book is written in a different time and culture, the human emotions were still very similar to mine, the more pieces of myself I saw, and the more I was able to see the lengths God is willing to go in order to remain connected to us.

In 2022 when my father, Bishop T. D. Jakes, passed the baton of the women's ministry Woman Thou Art Loosed (WTAL) to me, I imagine that it felt very similar to the moment when God highlighted Mary as one who was favored among women. The angel had not even told her what she was favored for, and she was concerned. Mary's initial response (or lack thereof) and the angel's thereafter confirm my suspicion:

> But when she saw [the angel], she was troubled at his saying, and considered what manner of greeting this was. Then the angel said to her, "Do not be afraid, Mary, for you have found favor with God." (Luke 1:29–30)

At the time, Woman Evolve was merely an infant in comparison to my father's ministry. WTAL had been a staple for women for almost four decades. As the date for its finale drew near, I anticipated an emotional farewell, not for my father to trust the anointing God had given me and grant me the sacred honor of carrying his legacy for women's freedom into a new frontier. In that moment, I felt the way Mary must have felt when God chose her to nurture and carry Jesus, an undeniable fresh move of the Spirit, into the earth: honored, nervous, redeemed, favored, afraid, but moving forward anyway.

We don't know much about Mary's motherhood journey

with Jesus, but we know that once she recovered from the shocking news of her life being upended, she embraced the change with joy and a hope that could come only from knowing heaven's resources were going to back her up.

Because I relate to Mary, my heart breaks for her when Jesus was on the cross. In John 19:25–27, we read:

> Now there stood by the cross of Jesus His mother, and His mother's sister, Mary the wife of Clopas, and Mary Magdalene. When Jesus therefore saw His mother, and the disciple whom He loved standing by, He said to His mother, "Woman, behold your son!" Then He said to the disciple, "Behold your mother!" And from that hour that disciple took her to his own home.

Mary had essentially finished her job, but it didn't have the sense of relief that it should bring.

It was always supposed to end with Jesus on the cross, but sometimes success feels like failure when it requires you to let go of who you once were. Mary, the mother of Jesus, who pushed Him from the womb and into the earth, was now watching as He transitioned from the earth and into the great unknown. Wouldn't it be natural for any mother to hope that God would save her child? Had God granted that request, Mary's hope would have thwarted God's ultimate plan of redemption.

At least Mary was armed with the knowledge that if she possessed that hope, it would have been directly against the will of

God. Most of us are hoping blindly because we don't know the ultimate will of God. But Mary was in a position so many of us find ourselves in when life has taken so many twists and turns that we don't know what to hope at all.

Not knowing what to hope for is not uncommon. Life is so complicated that you can often see the beauty and pain in either direction.

Think of Mary's situation. If Jesus lived, the world would have no Savior. If He died, Mary would have no son. John 3:16 says, "For God so loved the world that He gave His only begotten Son." It doesn't say anything about Mary's stance. If you've ever wondered whether you should hope the marriage repairs or ends, if the child should hit rock bottom or finally find her wings, or if you should direct your hope to build or to find contentment with where you are, you can relate to Mary in this moment.

The tension of this moment and the unsolicited command that Jesus gave her is a reminder to me of Jeremiah 29:11. When one of the primary roles of Mary's identity was coming to an end, Jesus gave her a future and a hope. She wasn't looking for it. As a matter of fact, she probably wouldn't have even known to ask for it, but Jesus gave her something to look toward beyond the pain of the moment. That new hope did not absolve the pain of what had come to an end, but it served as a reminder that hope and pain can live in the same space.

If you have experienced an unspeakable devastation that has consumed your heart with grief, you may think that you have to let the pain go in order to embrace hope. What if I told you that you don't have to choose? Receiving hope does not have to come at the expense of rushing through your valid pain. When you acknowledge the ways that God has allowed hope to meet you in dark seasons, it reminds whatever is holding you captive that you are not in it on your own.

I feel a little hope rising for you already.

HUNGRY FOR HOPE

1. What does the word *hope* mean to you? How do you use it in everyday conversation?
2. What power does hope have to change your mindset or influence your actions?
3. How has God carried you in the past? Do you believe He can do it again in the future?

FIVE
PUSH PAST SURVIVAL

I was always the youngest mom when it came to attending events or activities with my son. Although I didn't walk around with a T-shirt declaring my teen-mom status, I can imagine that it was pretty obvious by the way I dressed and carried myself that I wasn't like the other moms. There's a permanent look of "I'm still trying to figure out this motherhood and adulting stuff" that is plastered on the face of a teen mom.

Fortunately, God really took it easy on me when He gave me my son Malachi. Having grown up together, Malachi and I possess a special bond. His patience with me while I learned to find my footing in adulthood could have only come from heaven. He not only treats me with honor and respect as his mother, but he's also been like a personal cheerleader rooting for me to win.

One of my favorite memories with him is from when he was in the eighth grade. His grade in history class depended on his participation and execution of a project that would be presented schoolwide. It's not unusual for schools to host large projects once or twice a year, but I was in over my head when I learned the theme. His class was charged with hosting a Scarborough Fair, and each child had to set up a station within the market.

We were living in Los Angeles at the time, and I'd just given birth to Ella. I'll be honest: I'd never heard of the Scarborough Fair, so I was intimidated. My intimidation was intensified by the forty-eight-hour window in which I learned of and had to help Malachi execute his project. I'm all for preteens being responsible for their own work, but they're often so stressed and overwhelmed that depending on them to relay accurate information in a reasonable timeline can be an unnecessary added stressor for the parent.

Of course, I was too competitive to throw in the towel or let him fail, so I rolled up my sleeves to learn more about what was expected. Evidently, Malachi was supposed to set up a tent with a table and some kind of handmade bread or snack to trade with other students. He needed to make his booth as historically accurate as possible, and that included his wardrobe selection for the day. I was so close to calling Malachi's teacher and pointing out that Black people were not exactly under the best conditions during the period when Scarborough Fairs were popular, and thus we would be declining participation in this little reenactment. Malachi swiftly asked me to put away my daishiki and unclench my fists so that I didn't embarrass him at school. So there I was, with Ella in her car seat hooked at my elbow, rolling a canopy tent I'd ordered from Amazon across a football field while Malachi followed closely behind, lugging our table and crafts.

I was already sweating by the time we arrived at our designated spot on the lawn. I placed Ella's car seat on the ground, put my hands on my hips, and let out a deep sigh. I thought getting everything to its location on the field would be the hard part, but I realized almost immediately that Malachi and I didn't know anything about setting up a canopy tent.

Adding to my frustration was the fact that there weren't any instructions for putting it together because who would buy a medieval canopy tent that they don't know how to erect? I could see the anxiety filling Malachi's eyes when he realized that we'd have to figure it out with all the other middle school students and parents as our audience. My daishiki wasn't looking too bad after all.

I took a deep breath, looked him in the eyes, and, with sheer determination, said, "If we can survive me having you at fourteen years old, we can figure out how to put up a tent." If there's ever a movie done about my life, this is the moment when I'd like the theme song from *Rocky* to start playing. I grabbed a cranky Ella from her car seat, went to YouTube, and my boy and I conquered yet another obstacle together. As much as we want hope to come in the form of a new opportunity, good news, or the people we do life with, there are some moments when the easiest way to access hope is to look within.

When you take the harvest of yesterday into the opportunities of today, you are reminded that you have survived stress, pain, busyness, and weariness before.

Empowered by Survival

Buried in your experiences are lessons about life that prepare you for your next test. In order to access those lessons, you must live with an awareness that God wastes nothing, so you shouldn't either. If you aren't careful, you will become so relieved to see a season of your life change that you don't take the harvest from that time with you. When you take the harvest of yesterday into the opportunities of today, you are reminded that you have survived stress, pain, busyness, and weariness before.

I want to help you hone the skill of using the triumph of previous obstacles as momentum to face present pressures. Too often, when a chapter of our lives comes to an end, we want to distance ourselves from it altogether. Sometimes the pain of that chapter's ending is too much to bear. Then there are other moments when the achievement of that previous chapter is so great that we aren't sure anything else will compare.

When this occurs, we seek to reestablish ourselves apart from our past. If the events of your life were a housing development, and each time you closed a chapter you started again as if the previous things never happened, your life would resemble an idyllic suburban community. No one who sees you now would be privy to what happened in the "home" your high school years built.

You might be thinking, *That's the whole point! I don't want anyone to know about that pain.* The issue with this is that you also disconnect yourself from the resiliency, creativity, and passion that existed then too. The goal is for each stage of our life to honor our hope history and to build on it.

David wrote in Psalm 61:3–4, "For You have been a shelter for me, a strong tower from the enemy. I will abide in Your tabernacle forever; I will trust in the shelter of Your wings." Isn't it interesting that David used the term "tower" to symbolize safety in God? I believe it's because David saw how God met him in the lowest moments of his life yet continued to build for him a fortress of protection. Every new experience brought a new level of awareness of God's faithfulness and David's gifting. The same is true for you. If you're willing to stop fleeing and starting over and instead choose to build and develop from right where you are, you'll discover how God can use every part of your life.

Don't get me wrong—I completely understand why it's so much easier to avoid the vulnerability of dissecting your past. A fresh start makes us feel that hope can be discovered only in what's new and not in what's left over. There are things you have witnessed in your life that have the ability to reveal a perspective that would strengthen you in areas where you feel inadequate. You have felt weak, confused, and insecure before. Having those feelings didn't kill you. They may have spooked you into stagnancy, but those moments did not take the air out of your lungs.

If you live your life afraid to relive an experience, you are selling yourself short. You can reach a stage in your life where you're able to say, "I will *never* go through that again." But it won't be because you're afraid. It will be because you are so full of wisdom and strategy from your hope history that the only way you'd go through that again is if you abandoned yourself.

Then there will be accounts of your history that arm you with the ability to say, "I may not want to experience this again, but if I had to, I know I could survive it." Or my personal favorite: "If I survived that, then I can face this." The evidence of your ability to survive the seemingly unsurvivable is beating in your chest right now.

Can we get all touchy-feely here for a minute? Place your hand on your heart. Take a deep breath. Think of a moment you were convinced you could not possibly survive. It could be a week ago or twenty years ago. Allow that moment to come back, and feel the worry and anxiety that came with it. Then, with your hand still placed over your heart, whisper aloud, "I'm still here." Let that truth truly penetrate into the depths of your soul until you experience a level of gratitude that can come only when you realize that God was faithful in preserving you even when you thought you were perishing.

We do ourselves a disservice when we shortchange our resiliency. So much of what makes our world bearable are the people who have harnessed the power necessary to make a way out of no way. We need to be reminded that it's possible to overcome suffering and come out on the other side with a fresh revelation about who God is and what we can do when we trust that God is for us.

There are several passages throughout the New Testament where the apostles drew a connection between suffering and glory. Walking with Jesus helped them to understand that being under attack only served to expand their reach. It's almost as if the worst thing their enemies could have done was allowed them to see that they could survive. From prison cells to shipwrecks, readers of Scripture journey with the disciples through harrowing circumstances. Their circumstances did not diminish their faith but rather strengthened it. They counted it as an honor to suffer as Christ did. They understood that those moments when they were suffering as Christ did were also opportunities for God's glory to be further revealed. When your goal is to see God's glory no matter the cost, not even the toughest situation feels like complete loss. I have found myself repeating, with tears streaming down my face, "God's going to get the glory out of this."

End in Hope

If you're like me and there are moments when you feel completely depleted from being in survival mode 24/7, maybe we can both take a lesson from the apostles. They seemed to have mastered the ability to keep in the forefront of their minds that survival is a pit stop, not the final destination.

In February 2020, our Women Evolve team went on a tour called Refuse to Lose. These nightly events were the ultimate girls' night out that ended with a transformational encounter with God. In preparation for the tour, we asked the women attending to submit stories to us about how they are refusing to lose. In Philadelphia, we received a story from a young woman who was battling cancer. She took a photo holding a sign that said Refuse to Lose while receiving her chemotherapy treatment.

I began following her journey on Instagram and, like thousands of others, became invested in praying for and supporting her while she was in the fight of her life. Diamonique and her husband, Marcus, generously shared every part of their journey with us. When they announced that she was in remission, we all celebrated as if we knew her personally.

What I found remarkable about Diamonique's story is that once she survived, she still invited us on her journey. We watched as she learned to love the different stages of her hair returning. When I saw her regaining enough strength to spend time in the gym, it inspired me to get moving too. We all became internet aunties the moment she announced her pregnancy. Even now, Diamonique and Marcus continue to share content that is centered on life after her fight.

Can you imagine if she had rung the bell, walked out of the treatment center, then shut down her page? Had they decided that the only thing that mattered was her survival, we would have missed the moment when her identity expanded beyond being a young woman who was fighting cancer. We've now been able to witness Diamonique as a business owner, mother, influencer, wife, daughter, and friend. It's obvious that she saw herself as more than just a woman who had a battle on her hands. She was a woman determined not just to hold hope in her heart but to actually hold it in her hands for others to see.

When we stay in survival mode, our hope remains only in our hearts. But bringing the hope of our hearts into our present moment requires that we commit not just to making it to the other side of the obstacle but actively planning who we will be when it's all said and done. Don't be so blinded by what it's going to cost to survive that you miss the opportunity to have vision for who you will be when, not if, this obstacle is under your feet.

Often throughout the New Testament, Jesus mentioned that He was headed to the cross, but He also made sure His followers knew that the cross wasn't going to be the end. This way of thinking apparently rubbed off on His disciples, because we see many of them discussing not just suffering but also the glory connected to suffering. You may need to let your mind start wandering in the direction of hope more than it wanders in the direction of fear. If your mind is going to be tripping either way, you might as well make it start moving toward a space that produces hope and not more fear.

You may be a survivor, and that's beautiful. But the question is this: Are you living with fullness again? Survivor's rehab is when we extract and transfer the wisdom from our battle and apply it with hope to our relationships and opportunities.

Remember our friend Paul, who had his physical eyes shut but the eyes of his expectation opened in Acts 9? In Romans 5:3–5, Paul gave us the perfect road map for moving from survival to applying hope. He wrote:

We also glory in tribulations, knowing that tribulation produces perseverance; and perseverance, character; and character, hope. Now hope does not disappoint, because the love of God has been poured out in our hearts by the Holy Spirit who was given to us.

Paul's walk with the Lord revealed to him this mystery: there is a reason to "glory in tribulations." Paul must have known that these Christians in Rome needed to understand that even though there are moments when tribulation seems like it's leading to a dead end, if they would pay attention to what's happening in them, they would see that tribulation is actually rebirthing them. It's rebirthing you too.

The Coast Is Clear

Part of the reason we get stuck in the perseverance stage is that it feels more empowering than vulnerability. There's a certain level of mental toughness and edge that makes determination feel empowering. Then we grow weary from always having to fight, and that acceptance turns into exhaustion. If you are tired from the constant cycle of battles you've faced, I challenge you to consider whether you have yet taken a moment to celebrate and receive hope from your survival.

I've never spoken to Diamonique about her experience, but

I get the feeling that part of the joy she allows us to witness in her life was cultivated by her making commitments when she was fighting cancer about how she would live when she won. It wasn't just a fleeting thought that she had, but it is something she activated once the coast was clear. What if I told you that the coast is clear? You may have some victories under your belt that you have not taken the chance to fully celebrate because you were forced to face the next big thing.

Maybe this moment is an invitation for you to a victory party that is long overdue. The gifts for this party cannot be purchased at a store, but they are valuable nonetheless. The gifts for this party are connected to who you became as a result of what you faced. I know you probably realize that had you not gone through what you went through, you would not be who you are today, but have you allowed that to give you hope for the unknowns of tomorrow?

There are certain things that ruffle other people's feathers that don't shake you because you've survived the unthinkable. You've had to spend so many nights wondering how you were going to make it that you know all too well how to communicate with someone who is in a dark time. You've cried more tears than your pillow could hold and still found a way to get out of bed. You aren't barely here or barely making it. You're either making it or you aren't, and the only people not making it are those who are no longer alive to tell their stories.

If you could've seen your previous struggle before it came

When you discover
the divine attributes of
God that could have
only been revealed
as a result of your
tribulation, you move
from development to
the labor and delivery
stage of hope.

your way, you would have done the moonwalk in the opposite direction. It blindsided you. It knocked the wind out of your sails. It took your breath away, but then right when you were shocked, still, and numb, your struggle became a womb. Only you get to choose if you'll allow God to develop you from here.

Activating faith is the beginning of the development process that transforms perseverance into character. When you discover the divine attributes of God that could have only been revealed as a result of your tribulation, you move from development to the labor and delivery stage of hope. From there, the only thing that's left is for you to push.

Push away doubt.
Push away fear.
Push away inadequacy.
Push away anxiety.

Whenever hurdles appear, you push them back with affirmations that can come through Scripture, a sermon, or revelation you received from your quiet time with God. I'll be honest: there will be some days when it takes *all* those things and more than one push. But each time you push, it's imperative that you remember that you're not on your own. God's power is backing up those words.

Like a woman giving birth, you may not be able to push alone. You may need a friend to hold you, a therapist to coach you, and a team to support you. Your commitment to pushing may destroy your pride. It may force you to say things you'd otherwise not say, but in the end, the push is worth you breaking out of your comfort zone so that you can break free from the restrictions of your struggle and embrace the limitless potential of hope.

Hope is an inside job, but the coast has to be clear for it to make its way to the surface. That means you will have to practice rehearsing to yourself that it is okay for you to no longer live life on the defense. It's okay for you to reposition your mindset from protection to progression. Yes, it makes you vulnerable, and at times it may even make you a target, but you feel like that anyway even though you're guarded. If you're still here, it's not because God needed someone to protect the leftovers. It's because God trusted that you could partner with Him and work the leftovers. If God's got hope for what's in you, then maybe you should too.

HUNGRY FOR HOPE

1. Muster your courage for a moment and look back on something you've previously suffered. What did you learn about God from those tribulations? Would you have been able to learn those same lessons without your suffering?
2. What perspectives have you gained from obstacles you've overcome?
3. What have you achieved beyond your imaginings? What has God done with your grief? How has He refused to waste your pain?

KNOW WHAT YOU'RE WORKING WITH

You never could have convinced me that I would one day become known for public speaking. If I'm honest, it's still not my absolute favorite thing to do. When I study and feel prepared for the moment, there's nothing else I'd rather do than share what God has given me to say to the person, organization, or community I'm in front of. Heavy emphasis on the words "God has given me" because if God doesn't give me anything, then my introvert is totally in control.

I get nervous when I'm speaking just about anywhere, but I'm most nervous when walking into a new environment. Part of my nerves are rooted in the fact that I don't know the place I'm walking into. There are some spaces that feel just like home and showing up as myself is a breath of fresh air. Then there are other spaces where telling my story is taboo for the culture of the room. But I never know what I'm going to get until I'm in the space.

When my nerves begin to get the best of me, I challenge myself not to be so concerned with how I'll be received in the room that I fail to take in the room. I begin to notice the countenance of the people who are hosting me and the posture of the people I'm serving. I notice what type of statements elicit a response and also what seems to force the audience into deep contemplation.

More importantly, I pray that God will allow me to see and love the people and myself the way that He does. When I see an audience as a pool of jurors who are deciding whether or not I can add value to them, I immediately feel nervous. Nothing alleviates the tension in my stomach like remembering that the human experience is complex and dynamic for each of us. There's always something that can connect us.

All of this must take place for me to avoid my most common mistake when preaching. I've got a tragic habit of getting in my head while I'm speaking instead of pouring from my heart. This is problematic because it's difficult to analyze a room and be open to how God would like to use you to serve the room at the same time. When I'm in my head, I see everything: the person texting, the child who's asleep, the person who was obviously dragged into the room and doesn't want to be there.

By the way, if you're wondering if the speaker notices when you slip out with your bag—this one does. I'd like to say I'm thinking the highest thought as you casually turn your back and slip away, but in my head I'm like, *Oh no! What did I say? I wonder if I offended them.*

I learned to get out of my head after preaching a few sermons where my words didn't come out coherently and my thoughts were so scattered I kept losing my train of thought. At least that's how I experienced it. This only happens when I am critiquing myself in the moment instead of trusting God.

I'm so glad God causes all things to work together because there have been countless moments when I just knew a message was ineffective and wanted nothing more than to turn into a puddle right there in front of everyone, but somehow God allowed my stumbling and bumbling to turn into just the words that someone needed. I know with certainty that only God is responsible for turning my powerless insecurity into potent prophecy. I guess, for Him, it's kind of like turning water into wine.

I've been fortunate enough to have an opportunity to return to events where I previously struggled my way through a message. The second time around always brings with it an advantage because I'm equipped with an understanding of the people in the room and the environment the host creates. The comfort of knowing what to expect eases my nerves and makes it easier to speak from my heart instead of my head.

Revisiting a familiar place comes with a confidence that you're not afforded the first time. If you've been there once, you have context for what to expect. It's similar to trying a recipe for the second time. You know how to tweak and modify it the next time you make it.

Performing any task for the first time can make you understandably excited and trepidatious. However, the second time gifts you with confidence that would have been impossible to have before because you're armed with a perspective and confidence about the process. You would think the phenomenon of the second time adding confidence would aid us on our spiritual and emotional journey of navigating life, but it doesn't.

I believe part of the reason that we aren't armed with the full measure of peace we could have when we're facing the unknown is because we didn't properly land in a place of hope from the last battle we faced. That's why we must become diligent in extracting the hope from perseverance.

The first time that you consider your hope history, it can make you feel afraid, excited, and nervous all at the same time. You aren't sure if the journey back to those moments will be worth the pain or if there's anything that can possibly be gained.

If we were being super-duper honest, we'd also admit that our worry is rooted in our inability to be fully convinced that we can trust that God's light is able to extend into the deep darkness that even we don't want to experience. When we find the courage to extract the hope from those experiences, it truly does change how we see everything. You must extract the hope from your past so that you can see the potential of your present.

You must extract

the hope from

your past so

that you can see

the potential of

your present.

Where You Are Now

In Romans 5:4, Paul identified *hope* as the final state we arrive at after perseverance. Hope is the glimmering jewel we mine from difficulty that increases our value. It is also available to us as a lens that can serve us as we observe and engage in the world around us. This sounds so simple, but I know firsthand how challenging it is to be hopeful when you are in a circumstance you've never been in before.

It may be your first time facing this new situation, but it is not your first time having to strap in and prepare to survive the unexpected. If you can recall the last time a situation got so challenging that all you wanted to do was rub your temples and go to bed, you'll also remember how God sorted things out in a way you could not have expected.

The greatest trick that your Enemy possesses is getting you to forget what you're working with so that you become distracted worrying about things that God has already taken care of. When you know what you're working with, you also know what you don't have to put up with. If there were a microphone in my head where my inner thoughts could be heard, I am certain you would ask for a refund for this book.

Sometimes I have to talk sense to myself. I have an incredible knack for being skeptical about anything good someone says about me and nurturing every judgment that comes my way. All that inner dialogue comes to an end when I finally tell myself,

"Now, girl, you're so worried about what they're saying that you haven't even asked God for His thoughts to rise to the surface."

Are you like me? Do you have moments when you get caught fighting the wrong enemy with the wrong weapons? You're negotiating with your fears instead of paying attention to your faith. It reminds me of our girl Eve in Genesis 3. She should have curved that serpent like a girl who is determined not to let another man waste her time. When you know what you're working with, you also know what you don't have to put up with.

Seeing all things through a lens of hope is the most liberating perspective you can have, and I want to help you get there. It requires that you think less about what you're up against and more about what your opposition is making you believe about God and yourself. When you dissect the thoughts that worry and fear are creating in your present circumstance, compare them to the truth about God's faithfulness and your ability to endure.

If God eased those worries and gave you a future and a hope, why would He quit now? God is not tired of showing up for you. God is not keeping tabs on how many times He's had to bail you out. God loves you so much that the only thing He desires is to be connected to you with no dilution. What makes sin so devastating is not just the toll it takes on your heart, mind, and soul, but the way it weakens your ability to access God's unlimited resources of creativity, strategy, peace, power, and love. I think it's time for someone to tap back in.

There is so much hope to be found in where you are now. The

hope is not just in where you are headed or in what's left behind. It is the commitment to seeing everything in your life the way God sees it. When that occurs, you've tapped into the ability to look at every circumstance, even the most concerning, with a possibility of hope.

This is not positive thinking. I don't want you out there faking it until you make it. If it hurts, you better say ouch. If you're mad, you should let it out. Some of us can't see any hope because the smudges of grief and frustration have blurred the way forward.

When you invited God into your circumstance, He took note of your pain, but only so He could comfort you and then work it into His master plan of getting you to a place of hope. God knows what He's working with, so He's not afraid of you bringing all of yourself into your relationship with Him. When you finally let it all out, you won't hurt God's feelings; you'll expedite your healing.

Just thinking about this stirs up my excitement for what God is going to do with the healed and hopeful version of you. Hope is not about being rooted in the practical; it's about depending on the supernatural. If you've been trapped in reason, I hope these words are sawing off the chains that have kept you bound. Now is not a time to be practical or logical. Now is a time to be overwhelmingly confident that hope is for the here and now.

Your hope may be lying dormant underneath the belief that being practical will serve you better in the long run. Let me remind you about one thing: there's nothing practical about our God! The Red Sea just standing straight up, a shepherd boy turning into a king, a young virgin woman becoming with child, lepers being healed, a little boy's lunch becoming a feast for thousands . . . Shall I go on? If being practical is draining your hope, then abandon practicality and get unapologetically hopeful about what God can do.

The disciples learned this firsthand and shared with us throughout the New Testament countless moments when they abandoned the customs and expectations of the time and dared to release what they were working with. You may have the facts, but don't let the facts have you. God doesn't work facts. God works His promises.

Hope Is a Lifestyle

After Jesus was crucified and resurrected, He charged His disciples with the Great Commission. It's recorded in Acts 1:8: "But you shall receive power when the Holy Spirit has come upon you; and you shall be witnesses to Me in Jerusalem, and in all Judea and Samaria, and to the end of the earth."

It's a glimpse into the faith Jesus has in the disciples to be witnesses of the undeniable power of God that Jesus walked in throughout His time on the earth. The charge was simple enough that they should have been able to take off without any trouble, but Jesus understood that their passion would be tested by opposition.

Prior to giving them clearance to carry out the commission, Jesus gave them a divine expectation to wait on the Holy Spirit. Why couldn't they just go? Because even though the hope they extracted from their past was powerful, without Jesus they ran the risk of not seeing the hope in the present. The Holy Spirit isn't just leading us to hope. The Holy Spirit is helping us to abound in hope so that we can see the invisible potential in every moment.

Romans 15:13 encapsulates how the Holy Spirit and hope can align in our souls and offer us the opportunity to settle into a place of trust and confidence. It says, "Now may the God of hope fill you with all joy and peace in believing, that you may abound in hope by the power of the Holy Spirit." When you have the Holy Spirit, you have the power to abound in hope. The Greek word translated as "abound" in this verse means abundant.

To be hopeless is to lack the hope that the Holy Spirit has the power to give you in abundance. We're not talking about a little bit of hope dangling in front of your face, but rather a per-petual consciousness that provides you joy and peace because you know the God of hope is working even if you're hurting. Possessing hope in the face of great obstacles is choosing to tap into the invisible potential of any given moment. Every moment is brimming with possibility for hope to arise, but only those with a trained eye can expose it and bring it forth.

This is why I cannot overstate the necessity for you to look

Every moment

is brimming with

possibility for hope

to arise, but only

those with a trained

eye can expose it

and bring it forth.

beyond the weary aftermath of survival and begin to tap into the remnants of hope that are left over. God knows how to develop that hope into a lifestyle and perspective that will make all the difference for you.

In Acts 2, the apostles Peter and John received the power of the Holy Spirit on the day of Pentecost after being in the upper room. Jesus had endured the cross, was resurrected, and walked the earth for forty days to finish tying up loose ends before He went to sit at the right hand of God. One of those loose ends was equipping the disciples with undeniable revelation of His anointing and mission. The disciples had been in training with Jesus for three years, but now they were finally about to take center stage. In order to be effective, they'd need to overcome doubt and truly see the earth the way that Jesus did.

Jesus saw hope everywhere He went. He declared the kingdom of heaven was at hand because He was full of hope that if the people joined Him, they would have everything they needed in this world and the next. Jesus was filled with so much hope that it hurt Him when He realized that there was more need for hope than there were people who were willing to do the work to become hopeful.

> Then Jesus went about all the cities and villages, teaching in their synagogues, preaching the gospel of the kingdom, and healing every sickness and every disease among the people. But when He saw the multitudes, He was moved with compassion

for them, because they were weary and scattered, like sheep having no shepherd. Then He said to His disciples, "The harvest truly is plentiful, but the laborers are few. Therefore pray the Lord of the harvest to send out laborers into His harvest." (Matthew 9:35–38)

The disciples were literally an answer to that prayer. They likely started walking with Jesus out of curiosity about the magnetic draw that was His spirit. But I'm sure they continued to walk with Jesus because of how He was unmoved by the condition of their oppression. If you're a history buff, you know that for a Jewish man living under Roman rule at that time, to begin declaring that the kingdom of heaven was at hand was audacious.

Rome was the superpower of the world, and the idea that there was a greater kingdom seemed unbelievable. Even more unbelievable was the notion that the kingdom that would overthrow Rome would derive from the significantly oppressed Jewish community. For Jesus, declaring this truth took more than just hope; it took confidence. He had so much confidence in what He was hoping for that it didn't matter whether it scared those who were against Him. Jesus saw invisible potential because the Holy Spirit was granting Him insight into the hope God had for the world.

Your hope may sound crazy based on what you've gone through. It may not make any sense at all considering what you're up against, but when you know what you're working with, there's nothing anyone can do to stop you. Jesus knew what He was working with, and He became so intently focused on what the earth could become that He was not dissuaded by the present condition of the world.

That level of audacious hope began rubbing off on the disciples, and shortly after Jesus ascended to heaven, we see the disciples moving with that same level of authority. One of my favorite accounts is in Acts 3, when Peter and John encountered the lame man at the gate called Beautiful. The lame man was simply minding his business at the temple gate, hoping to receive some change for the day. He was hoping for the practical.

Then Peter and John came over to him. They were fueled by a lens of hope, and as a result they saw invisible potential for the lame man. Famously, they told him, "I don't have any money, but I'm working with something that will change your life!" (v. 6, author's paraphrase). If you've ever gone through a season of extreme brokenness and come out on the other side of wholeness with a fresh revelation of who you are, you cease to be desperate for any ol' body to complete you. Instead, you come to a place where you realize that you are the prize because you can finally see clearly what you're working with.

I challenge you not to take the hope that remains and tuck it away for safekeeping. Instead, I want you to bring it to the forefront of your mind and allow it to be the filter you use when you see and hear all things. Hope is not a limited resource. Romans 15:13 says that the God of hope wants to bring you to a place of joy and peace in believing so that your hope replaces worry, anxiety, and fear of the unknown. If the only thing you know is that you're working with the God of hope, then that's all you need to face the pain of yesterday, maximize the potential of today, and trust the promises of tomorrow.

HUNGRY FOR HOPE

1. How can you try today to see things the way God sees them?

2. What change happens in your mind and heart when you begin to look for the possibilities instead of the potential obstacles ahead of you?

3. How does it feel to know that Jesus Himself has faith in you to carry out His divine mission?

SEVEN
PUT YOUR HOPE TO WORK

There are quite a few stories in the Bible that move me deeply. They usually center on characters who struggled to reclaim their identity and connection with God after disappointing themselves or others. Peter is one of those characters whose story resonates with my own. He was minding his business when Jesus approached him with a job opportunity. Low-key, Jesus' initial pitch would've sounded like a multilevel marketing scheme if we heard it today—a little far-fetched but also undeniably intriguing.

Peter was a fisherman. This was a common and straightforward profession at the time. But when Jesus approached Peter and his brother Andrew while they were fishing, He didn't lure them with promises of power, riches, or fame. Jesus simply told them, "Follow Me, and I will make you fishers of men" (Matthew 4:19).

It turned out that Peter wasn't just a good fisherman; he was an incredible follower of Jesus. Peter was a rock star disciple and immediately became a part of Jesus' inner circle. Jesus had twelve disciples, but did you know that even among the Twelve there were three men He held especially near? Peter was a part of that inner circle of three, and he bore witness to irrefutable evidence of Jesus as the Son of God.

I love that Jesus took what Peter already knew well and introduced a purpose that would build upon that. When God begins to reveal how you can serve what He's doing in the earth, it won't require you to be someone you're not. God will not call you to something that your history has not prepared you for in some way.

Peter was the first disciple to be affirmed in his ability to hear directly from God long before the Holy Spirit visited the upper room on the day of Pentecost. This moment occurred when Jesus asked His disciples who they said He was. Peter answered, "You are the Christ, the Son of the living God" (Matthew 16:16). His response prompted Jesus to affirm him in his identity and to grant him more access, trust, and authority than any other disciple. Jesus told Peter,

> Blessed are you, Simon Bar-Jonah, for flesh and blood has not revealed this to you, but My Father who is in heaven. And I also say to you that you are Peter, and on this rock I will build My church, and the gates of Hades shall not prevail against it. And I will give you the keys of the kingdom of heaven, and whatever you bind on earth will be bound in heaven, and whatever you loose on earth will be loosed in heaven. (vv. 17–19)

God will not

call you to

something that

your history has

not prepared you

for in some way.

One would think that, with all that affirmation, Peter would've been the one disciple Jesus could count on no matter what. Well, one would be wrong because the moment the kitchen got hot, Peter got ghost. (Sorry about that; my roots started showing in the last sentence.) Essentially, when Jesus was arrested and facing persecution, Peter was not just nowhere to be found; he denied knowing Jesus altogether. Three times!

When Jesus was resurrected and needed to inform the disciples, He had an angel reveal the news to the two women at his tomb. The angel said, "Do not be alarmed. You seek Jesus of Nazareth, who was crucified. He is risen! He is not here. See the place where they laid Him. But go, tell His disciples—and Peter—that He is going before you into Galilee; there you will see Him, as He said to you" (Mark 16:6–7).

Isn't it powerful that when it was time for Jesus to gather the disciples, the angel specifically said Peter's name? This isn't special treatment. It's because Peter was so disappointed with himself that he no longer considered himself a disciple. The fisher of men had gone back to just being a fisherman.

When Rome apprehended, tortured, and then crucified Jesus, it seemed that they had been successful at squelching His impact. Even the disciples were scared into stagnancy. The finality of His body being placed in the tomb seemed to signal that all hope had been lost. His resurrection should have been the moment when faith was restored and the mission continued.

Based on Peter's love for Jesus, I'm sure the resurrection

produced relief and shame: relief that his Friend was alive and the gospel would continue to spread, but also a deep shame from denying Jesus that prevented Peter from returning to the position he once held. Regardless of how unworthy he may have felt when Jesus was resurrected, Jesus still called for Peter to meet Him in Galilee. Even when we back away, we serve a God who doesn't mind calling us back.

Jesus' exchange with Peter in John 21 wasn't a conversation for closure or a mea culpa from Peter. Instead, it was Jesus challenging Peter to overcome his previous mistakes and failures and to channel the hope of the resurrection toward serving what matters the most to Jesus.

The hope we extract from our past changes our perspective, but it's not until we put our hope to work that we partner with God to bring pieces of heaven to earth. It's not enough to hold hope within. You have to actively seek ways to spread hope in all that you do. If you're going to leave a lasting impression, how can you make sure that it's not about making yourself look good but rather leaving the moment more hopeful than it was before you entered?

Work the Word

Jesus was the master of seeing hope in the most hopeless individuals and situations. Part of why He was able to do that is that He

If hope is the lens,

then love is the

frame that keeps

hope in its place.

functioned in a realm of love. If hope is the lens, then love is the frame that keeps hope in its place. When you have a revelation of how deeply loved you are by God, you will also understand that God does not place His love where there is no hope.

God sees you through the lens of hope that is held in place by the frame of love. That frame cannot be broken by your mistakes, sins, or shortcomings. God's love is undeniable, unchangeable, and unbreakable. God does not give up hope as it relates to who you have the potential to become because God cannot separate you from His love.

In John 21, Jesus asked Peter three times whether he loved Him. Not to get all Tina Turner, but what does love have to do with Peter's inability to get back to seeing hope after disappointment? Everything!

We all know that cheesy couple who are so in love that they make even the most ridiculous and mundane tasks a joy. Low-key, that couple is probably my husband and me. No matter how bad a situation is, or has the potential to become, if my husband and I are facing it together, I have hope that it will leave us with a tighter connection, a few inside jokes, and a deep knowledge that we can face difficulty as a unit and come out on the other side. If you have not known love well, hope will always be fleeting, but if you were to ever understand how much hope God sees in you, it would soothe your soul and awaken your confidence to take action.

Jesus gave Peter a word in John 21 that was meant to get

Peter's life back on the right track. I think we can all relate to the discouragement that comes from feeling out of place. Have you ever been in that space and then received a message from a book, sermon, or podcast that made you feel alive? When God sends you a word for your life, you have to be willing to do what it takes to put the hope to work. Receiving that word comes down to not just believing that it was a good idea or an inspirational thought but seeing it as a truth that needs to transform your mind.

The word God sends to you is meant to unlock the version of you who can change things in the earth. If you don't work your hope, then hopelessness wins. But when you work your word, it shifts your world. You may be thinking it would be useless to embark on a journey of change because the people around you are stuck in their ways. You'd be surprised what happens when you begin to show up differently. It can inspire other people to do the same with their lives or give you the confidence you lack to move independent of other people's pace.

Peter eventually began to work the promise Jesus gave Him, and as a result, he became known for his ability to speak with power, authority, and boldness, and to perform miracles. The same man who almost gave up became a man God could depend on. I desire to be the type of woman God can depend on. I have plenty of reasons why God should choose someone else, but if God throws a word in my direction, I'll do all I can to make sure it doesn't fall to the ground.

I have always found that the word God gives me often

confronts my inner way of being. While most people want a word about who they will become or what they will possess, we must make sure we don't miss the words that challenge who we are and how we function now.

I won't lie—the illumination of our deficiency is rarely comfortable, but it is necessary. God sends conviction to get you one step closer to who you can become. Obeying conviction paves the way to receiving God's vision for your life.

It's no secret that I wear wigs. Underneath the wigs my hair is braided to my scalp in a pattern that has culturally been reserved for men. I don't wear my wig 24/7, but I try not to slide it off randomly when I'm in the room with my husband. I always give him a warning like, "Your lady is about to turn into a dude real quick." He used to get on my nerves because the moment I took off the wig, he'd start talking about how beautiful I looked.

I'd roll my eyes and cock my head in disbelief because there ain't no way I could look beautiful. One day, I stopped rolling my eyes and cocking my head when he said it. My disagreement was rooted in insecurity and improbability, but as I was tapping into a hope that I could love myself in every stage and phase, I realized that I needed Touré's words to call me to a higher level of thinking and existing.

Don't cancel out the words God sends out of fear. Find a way to put that hope to work. Instead of rolling my eyes and being annoyed by the idea that I could possibly be beautiful in my raw state, I've learned to strike a cute pose and pucker my lips when

I take off my wig. I'm learning to lean into the actions that make my hopes tangible.

Activate Your Hope

I want you to begin seeing your hope as less like a wish that is out of your control and more like a destination that is within your ability to move toward. When we see our hope only as an event that might someday occur in our lives, we miss the opportunity to tap into the character that makes room for hope to become a reality. Having a baby, meeting your soulmate, buying a home, climbing the corporate ladder, and starting a business are among the hopes many women possess that are centered around moments. Anyone who has ever had such a hope and then had the experience recognizes that the fulfillment of that hope is filled with gratitude, amazement, and wonder. Then there's a moment when the thing you once hoped for becomes a staple you can depend on, and it loses some of its sparkle.

When we consider instead how experiencing this event will transform our perspective of ourselves, God, or others, we unearth an even deeper hope. From that place of gratitude, our hope becomes less about an occurrence and more about a transformation we want to experience. Who will we be on the other side of that hope, and can we tap into that person now?

A woman may desire to become a mother for any number

of reasons, but one of the most beautiful reasons is the desire to experience protecting, serving, and enjoying another human from infancy to adulthood. There are many women I know personally who would be incredible mothers, but their hope has not yet been fulfilled. I pray often that God would comfort their hearts on their journey and lead them to His perfect will for their lives. I also pray that they would be able to experience their desire to protect, serve, and enjoy another human, even if it's not in the way they originally intended.

When you begin to activate the hope of who you can become outside of the event that you feel will propel you into the becoming, you will begin to realize that hope is not as far away as it seems. How can you begin to make choices today as if the hope for tomorrow is already present? That's taking your hope from inside your heart and allowing it to become a seed in the earth. You will be able to say to yourself, "I may not yet have what I'm hoping for, but I have hope in whom I'm becoming."

Maybe it has become clear that your spirit could heal if you were able to release your anger and connect with a more vulnerable way of living. If that's your hope, then what can you enact today that puts your hope to work? Some of my favorite miracles in Scripture occurred when Jesus helped someone who was in need to identify their desire and then put in work to make it happen. For example, in John 5:6, He asked a sick man, "Do you want to be made well?" When the person said yes, God provided an instruction that would produce the result.

I could write a book about the moments when God did something in my life that overwhelmed me with His goodness. I know that I didn't earn it or deserve it. I also recognize that I don't have to downplay that my participation played a role. I had to fight the feelings of inadequacy, study, create boundaries, practice, apologize, and forgive to keep God's hope for my life in reach.

There's something to be said about the statement, "God helps those who help themselves." Maybe we can change the words? "God helps those who hope themselves." I like that because it serves as a reminder that when our hope marries God's help, restoration is sure to occur.

Incremental changes in our lives can have a monumental impact. Whether your hope is big or small, the more you can dissect the hope and align your life to reflect the preparation for what you're hoping for, the better. Create the boundaries, save the money, start the program, and honor every aspect of your health. Do all that is within your power to make room for God's plan, not just so that it's clear to you but also so that your heart can be positioned in such a way that God's plan is acceptable to you.

Guard Your Heart

So how do we break the tie to the moment we're hoping for and rest in the becoming that is connected to our hope instead? There have been so many projects and desires that I've wanted to experience, and the anticipation of wondering whether God would answer my prayer filled my soul with a lot of anxiety. I've heard the scripture about not being anxious for anything many times. I've had moments when it helped to remind me to trust God, but I've also had other moments when it did not appease my worry at all. In preparing for my year of hope, I read this scripture in its entirety and saw for the first time how we can complement our desire for an experience with our desire to have peace regardless.

In Philippians 4:6–7, the apostle Paul said, "Do not be anxious about anything, but in every situation, by prayer and petition, with thanksgiving, present your requests to God. And the peace of God, which transcends all understanding, will guard your hearts and your minds in Christ Jesus" (NIV).

I looked at this scripture in its original language and learned so much about the intent for the verse, but initially I stumbled because the words "prayer" and "petition" felt like synonyms. Almost as soon as the thought crossed my mind, I felt convicted. If your prayer life has been reduced to petitions, then your connection with God is being underutilized.

Prayer is not the place where we come and hand God our list of desires. It is the place where we lay out our hearts before the Lord and receive His heart. Prayer is the sacred exchange of our weakness for His strength. It is how we communicate and receive God's presence. The Greek word translated as "prayer" in Philippians 4:6 actually means "worship."

Most people believe that worship is reduced to a moment in a church service or a song captured to play when your soul needs it the most. While it is all of that, I see worship as a heart posture rooted in the acknowledgment and pursuit of God's presence. Cultivating a lifestyle of worship occurs when we remind ourselves as often as possible that we are constantly in the presence of God. This is not an easy task, because our attention is often divided by the demands of the moment.

This is not a suggestion for you to be, as the old church folks used to say, "so heavenly minded that you are no earthly good." Instead, I'm imploring you to recognize that by the sheer reality of how full your life is with responsibilities, stress, and fun, you may not always recognize how close God is to you at any given time.

He is in the doctor's office.
He is in the carpool line.
He is at the kitchen table.
He is in the trauma counselor's session.

Prayer is where we practice this consciousness. There are some people who recite a daily prayer that gets them to that place, but my prayer life begins with a deep reverence and acknowledgment of God. Have you ever looked at a vast ocean with the recognition that there's an entire universe underneath the surface and thought, *You can't tell me God isn't real?*

What about watching a woman go from the early stages of pregnancy to holding her baby in her arms? There's nothing like that moment when you realize that God created her body to develop cells into a cranky baby swaddled in a blanket.

The sky teeming with stars? A yes to a dream you were convinced should have been no? An unexpected opportunity that became a monumental blessing? There are countless moments that my spirit knows, even when my mind is occupied with the battle of faith or fear, that God is real.

When I pray, I recall those moments to my spirit, and my mind is rendered to a hush. That is the starting heart posture for my prayer. You should keep a list of wonder in your phone that can quickly bring your spirit to the forefront when your mind is in disarray. It's a beautiful way to begin prayer because it is a reminder of the intentionality of God.

When we bring our petitions to God, it creates a great sense of humility and trust. You may not know how God will acknowledge your request, but you can trust that His answer will be drenched with the same intentionality that set the ocean in motion, holds the sun in its place, and creates new life.

When you find a way to truly rest in that ever-present connection, you can be assured that "the peace of God, which transcends all understanding, will guard your hearts and your minds in Christ Jesus" (Philippians 4:7 NIV).

HUNGRY FOR HOPE

1. Have you ever received a word from God? If so, what was it, and how did you respond? If you would like God to send you a word, make a plan to spend some time with Him in prayer.

2. You have to actively seek ways to spread hope in all that you do. If you're going to leave a lasting impression, how can you make sure that it's not about making yourself look good but rather leaving the moment more hopeful than it was before you entered?

3. Have you ever felt discouraged and out of place and then received a message from a book, sermon, or podcast that made you feel alive? How did that change your mindset?

EIGHT
HOPE SPEECH

There is an ongoing debate in the Western world, particularly in North America, regarding hate speech. Arguments have ensued around the laser-thin line between freedom of expression and hate speech. The line of demarcation and what qualifies as hate speech has been long debated and will continue to be debated until Jesus comes.

I pray that God never calls me to be an elected official because my policies and campaign would basically come down to drink your water, mind your business, and stay ready so you don't have to get ready. When I say that's it, I mean that with my whole heart.

Now that we have established how inadequate I am to be an elected official, I will say that I've been thinking quite a bit about hate speech. I am not sure I could define it in my own terms. But in my study of what qualifies as hate speech, I ran across a definition from the United Nations I'd like to share: "any kind of communication in speech, writing or behavior, that attacks or uses pejorative or discriminatory language with reference to a person or a group on the basis of who they are, in other words, based on their religion, ethnicity, nationality, race, colour, descent, gender or other identity factor."[5]

With this definition in mind, I can see how the rhetoric of the past and present fits into this category. The need to categorize communication as hate speech became necessary because it began to provoke violence against a particular group.

Words in the mouth of the wrong person can be as deadly as a trigger in the hands of a hate-filled individual. Defining hate speech became necessary to hold people accountable who may not have performed the act of violence but initiated it with verbiage that lit a flame that created an inferno.

I admire the desire to see individuals who engage in hate speech be held accountable. When I was growing up, you couldn't just say anything. And if you were going to say something, you had to watch your tone to make sure it didn't offend the ears of the adult you were speaking with.

"Watch your mouth" is one of those phrases that has withstood the test of time. It's truly a testament to the power that words and communication possess. Whoever said, "Sticks and stones may break my bones, but words will never hurt me" must have been the person who was spewing harmful words.

I think we can all attest to the moments when harsh words

stung much deeper and longer than the pain of physical wounds. Attempts to diminish the power of words lower the barrier for what is deemed acceptable and appropriate not just in our political climate and local communities but also in our friendships, families, and inner dialogue.

We often hear those who engage in harmful language excuse it as just the way they are, as if that absolves them of the responsibility and impact their words have on others. It's so important that we take the time to assess whether the intent of our communication is missed because of our delivery.

The heart posture of worship may be helpful in assisting us in measuring the love that is in our words. Did your words to a person whom God loves help the journey of wholeness He desires them to experience? Or did you allow your pride, fear, or pain to take the microphone instead?

This is not a judgment because I once took pride in using my mouth as a sword and daring anyone who betrayed me to be prepared for the slicing and dicing of a lifetime. That was a little Eve "know better, but don't do better" energy that I wore as a shield to protect myself. That energy is still in me and will rise up in a heartbeat if you try one of my loved ones.

However, I have learned to temper that fire with the reminder that God has literally allowed my words to collide with His Spirit to help heal, redeem, and encourage those whom He loves. It's hard to pop off with your mouth when you feel a conviction to allow heaven to touch earth through your words.

I want you to begin

to speak like the

person you're

hoping to become,

not the person you

invented to survive.

As often as possible, we must take inventory of the words we've spoken and make sure they align with our ultimate desire to speak like we're the person we're hoping to become. This can happen only through self-reflection. We must take the time to replay conversations that may have been awkward, tense, or required vulnerability, and assess whether the best version of ourselves showed up in the moment. I want you to begin to speak like the person you're hoping to become, not the person you invented to survive.

I hope you don't feel a sense of pressure with that. It should motivate you to begin moving in the direction of your purpose. The options are not do it perfectly or don't do it at all. You are not always going to get this right because you're human, and you've practiced the reflex to be negative or defensive for years. However, the moment you realize that your words no longer align with your values, you have a responsibility to mitigate the impact with an acknowledgment of where you fell short, an apology, and a commitment to grow.

The charge I just gave you is not my favorite thing. As a matter of fact, it really does sound better than it feels, especially when a person truly crossed a line. Their offense should not have the power to draw you out of your character. There is not a person or situation that is worthy of you reverting to a version of yourself that you no longer want to be. An apology for your role is not a license for the behavior to continue.

By all means, maintain the boundary, but don't allow it to

come at the expense of your character or integrity. It is possible to be wrong about how you said something but not be wrong about what you said.

I do enough work with women to understand how much the words of trusted people within their circle, from childhood friends to family members to coworkers, continue to cause harm that they're trying to undo. If you can relate to the journey of unrooting the words of others that created a harmful perception of love, faith, and trust, then my heart goes out to you. I wish you had experienced better. I hope that you're at a place where you can give yourself the better you deserve.

It's Not Funny

There's a weird stage of adolescence where inappropriate jokes and language become normalized. Children, often too engrossed with the pursuit of social acceptance to understand the responsibility they have to be good stewards of their words, engage in conversations and jokes that come at the expense of the well-being and esteem of their peers.

I really do try to be the cool mom when my daughter is sharing with me the latest phrase that has swept her classroom. It's usually something eye-rollingly obnoxious (yes, I made up a word). I try to grin and bear it while she tells me a story that includes this new phrase. When she's finished, I make sure that

I find a way to inform and expand her use of the words. I let her know how time or experience may reveal that the same words used as a joke could be a trigger to someone else or even herself soon.

If she didn't understand that when I shared it with her, then she got an understanding when the usual banter of the class turned into derogatory conversations about teenage mothers and how "stupid, avoidable, and dumb" it is for a girl to end up pregnant. My daughter was not amused. She stepped out of the classroom and tried to find a way to express to them that there are some things that are just not funny.

I didn't think much about the comments when she shared the story with me. I saw it as an opportunity for her to express herself and provide insight into how much more nuanced life is than her classmates may understand. I've done enough healing and therapy not to be offended by other people's ignorance.

There was a time in my life when people would share those views in the room with me. Sometimes the people had knowledge that they were talking about my experience, and sometimes they did not. Even when those conversations weren't taking place, I could still hear their thoughts confirming my insecurities at night.

Hate speech is not just about the conversations we direct toward others. It's also the narrative we allow to take up space in our heads. There are a few highlights of the United Nations' definition of *hate speech* that I believe are worthy of discussion:

"any kind of communication ... that attacks ... a person ... on the basis of who they are."[6]

Is the narrative that guides your philosophy about your body, potential, roles, and talents affirming you? Or do you possess a narrative that insists on attacking you based on your insecurities? If so, maybe we should find some time to shift our focus from the hate speech that is spewed around us and instead take a dive into the sea of you. Sis, are you hating on yourself?

Internal hate speech is subtle because it's rooted in evidence of who we believe ourselves to be. Remember that definition? It highlights "any type of communication," including those silent thoughts running through your head that are having a conversation with your destiny. They are challenging you on the basis of who you once were or what you don't have.

If you've ever thought that you're not smart enough, good enough, big enough, small enough, loud enough, quiet enough, pretty enough, or strong enough, then I'm talking to you. You've got to recognize that the hate speech in your head is keeping you from releasing the hope speech that will make God's vision for your life a reality.

Oftentimes these thoughts are not random. They are the aftermath of circumstances that left you uncertain. A narrative rooted in lived experiences is hard to break, but not impossible. You must be willing to ask yourself if the language you're utilizing is helping you or hurting you.

If you don't readily know the answer, consider if you're being further restricted or limited based on your current thought process. If the words in your head are telling you what you can't do or who you can't become, then those words aren't from God.

Whenever Jesus was setting captives free, He didn't invite them into healing by telling them what they couldn't do. Instead, Jesus lured them with a proposition of freedom from what ailed them. A genuine God encounter provides you with a glimpse of what's possible for you that is so enticing that He doesn't have to tell you who you aren't; He just makes you hungry to become.

What if your communication, internal or external, is the barrier that's keeping your hope from coming alive?

Let It Live

There will be moments when your expectations are transformed and your values are refined. Early on, when I presented my business ideas to potential partners and friends, I didn't expect for them to get it. I expected rejection. But as I learned to truly trust who I am in God, I began to expect expansion from collaboration and not restriction.

Your expectations and values are going to change the more you pursue God's identity. When this occurs, it is likely that your hopes will change too. Not every hope is rooted in wholeness. As you begin to walk out your life with God's vision for your identity as the goal, it will become much easier to trust your hopes.

There's a difference between the spiritual evolution of you changing your hopes and you forcing your hope to die because it seems too unrealistic. I'm talking about the moments when we kill our hope before hoping for it kills us.

What do you do, though, when God makes it clear that He's creating an opportunity for that hope to be revived? When God sends a word to you that feels like a defibrillator to something you allowed to die, it can send your mind into a spiral. The tailspin of thoughts is not as toxic as the hate speech we've discussed. Let's consider this doubt speech. It is rooted in skepticism and can be just as dangerous as hate speech. Skepticism is the undoing of faith.

When you become skeptical about what God says is possible, it keeps you from obtaining the faith that makes the impossible possible. You would not be the first woman who had to deal with skepticism as it relates to destiny. Consider Abraham's wife, Sarah, when she overheard God's news that she would have a baby:

> He said, "I will certainly return to you according to the time of life, and behold, Sarah your wife shall have a son." (Sarah was listening in the tent door which was behind him.) Now Abraham and Sarah were old, well advanced in age; and Sarah had passed the age of childbearing. Therefore Sarah laughed within herself, saying, "After I have grown old, shall I have pleasure, my lord being old also?" (Genesis 18:10–12)

Sarah could not convince herself to believe that God could change her situation. She adapted to the language of her circumstance so much that even when God was trying to break her out of it, she could not let go.

Did you notice in the text that Sarah "laughed within herself"? You think because you haven't said it aloud that God doesn't know you're living in doubt? Heaven hears what your heart is whispering. You're going to have to let your spirit take over so that heaven's hope language can permeate the places where doubt is taking up space.

I don't want you to miss the miracle connected to your life because your insides can't align with what God is promising. On the surface, God was offering Sarah the opportunity to produce a child in her old age, but internally God was offering her an opportunity to produce fresh faith. Her laughter reflected the state of her faith, but God was so gracious that He did not abandon her in her disbelief.

Sometimes God speaks to us in the language of hope to our hearts, but we're so convinced that the window of opportunity has passed that we can't match God's language regarding what's possible. If God could have bypassed Sarah's doubt, His words would have filled her with praise and gratitude that God had not forgotten her. But because she'd been reduced to doubt, she couldn't discern that God was giving her faith an opportunity to increase.

God is speaking to us in the language of hope, but we've

been conditioned by our community or insecurity to comprehend only doubt. Did you know it's possible to become so accustomed to negative opinions that when someone offers you hope or affirmation, you don't know how to receive it and don't trust that you can believe it? I challenge you to begin speaking and hearing God's language louder than you do your doubt.

When God sent Sarah a word, it highlighted her internal doubt. But God called out what she thought she was holding within. Every now and then, you need someone to call you out so that you can come to terms with how skeptical you've become about the thing you once hoped for. This moment in Scripture is where we receive one of the most recognizable verses about God's character. It's Genesis 18:14: "Is anything too hard for the LORD? At the appointed time I will return to you, according to the time of life, and Sarah shall have a son." Those first seven words are a rhetorical question because the answer is no.

If you're going to have an inner dialogue about the matters of your heart, make sure you remember that when everything is said and done, if you've invited God's presence to lead you and guide you, it's going to work out. That means you can respond to your worries, doubts, and fears with the seven words that will settle your soul: "Is anything too hard for the LORD?" Like Sarah, there will be a time when what God said becomes what you hold.

Declare God's Hope

We've got a tricky habit of not wanting to speak our hopes out loud. The fear of embarrassment if it doesn't come to pass or the accountability from people in our circle leaves us silent about legitimate desires. Remaining silent about your hope does not secure its future.

I know that not everyone can handle your desires and that you don't want to expose a hope that means a lot to you to a person or group who may disregard it. But pretending that you don't want something that you truly do fragments your confidence.

I can't tell you how many people feel unworthy of their spouses, careers, and families because they denied wanting them when what they really wanted to avoid was having it and then losing it. It's okay to admit that, if God is willing, your heart is still open to receive what you're afraid to want.

Also, I've got to let you know it's okay to change your mind. Maybe there was a time in your life when you truly desired partnership, but now you've reached a stage where what you really desire is to partner with the most divine version of who you are. You need a community that is nimble enough to change with you as life changes. Your tribe should be able to handle the moments when your hopes have shifted without punishing you for needing something different.

You are not a statue. You are a living, breathing creature on a journey of discovering who you are in God and shedding who you once were. This journey ensures that Psalm 37:4—"Delight yourself also in the Lord, and He shall give you the desires of your heart"—will become your portion. God is going to give you new desires as He introduces you to the you He's known. What you once rejected and denied, you now may find yourself in pursuit of.

If you don't own that truth, you're going to have a secret life of hope and a loud life of doubt. You own this truth by disagreeing when someone projects a different narrative from the secret one of your soul. You own this truth by sharing it with others and asking for them to add their faith to your own. You wear your hope on your sleeve like a badge of honor so that anyone you encounter understands that your hope has not been dismissed. Gone are the days of deflecting your desires: since you doubt you can have it, you live like you don't want it but pray that God will send it your way. No, ma'am. We don't have time for that. Jesus is coming back at any given moment, and we want Him to find you in truth. It's time for you not just to own your hope but to declare it.

Correct the misconceptions you created or the misperceptions of others. Your strength is in the integrity of your being, not in the places where you've been accepted.

I had to take this spoonful of medicine myself. Everyone who knows me knows that I like to sit my tail down at my house. I want you to invite me places. I even want to tell you I'm coming, but when I'm at home and I start sizing up the energy required to go out, I decide the only energy I'm exerting will be with my

It's time for

you not just

to own your

hope but to

declare it.

two thumbs sending a text that I'm not coming. When I travel, I get in and out as quickly as humanly possible because I want to get home as quickly as humanly possible.

One day I was sitting at the dinner table, and our family and friends were talking about the possibility of me traveling the world and preaching. Someone who knows me well said, "Sarah does not want to be traveling the world exhausted and preaching." A laughter of agreement erupted in the room. I joined the chorus, but my insides refused. The thing is, I *do* want to travel the world preaching to whomever God sends my way. I want to do my part in fulfilling the Great Commission.

I figured it didn't matter because it was all jokes anyway. Still, later that night, I picked up the phone and connected with the person directly. My words were simple: "Actually, I do want to travel the world preaching. It's one of the things I long to do." They responded, "Well, I'll add my faith to yours." It gave me the comfort of knowing that I wasn't the only one praying for that hope to become a reality.

When you own your hope and share it publicly, you give other people permission to join you on the journey. You may be avoiding someone's contamination by keeping it to yourself, but you might also be missing someone's confirmation and affirmation. Countless times in Scripture we're exposed to the power of what happens when people are gathered together with a unified focus and goal. The only way to protect your hope from being hijacked by fear is to own it with faith and trust God's plan.

HUNGRY FOR HOPE

1. What is something someone has said to you recently that filled you with confidence and hope?
2. How can you strategically use your own words to spread hope to others this week?
3. How is hope the antidote to doubt? What does doubt do to your outlook and mindset the longer you dwell in it?

NINE

CONTAGIOUS HOPE

In chapter 1, I mentioned that I've found a health routine that works for my lifestyle and doesn't feel like a chore. In exchange for giving up on quick fixes, I've had to make peace with the reality that my journey to strength and optimum health will require me to embrace the mentality that slow and steady wins the race.

I was a sucker for the "Lose Ten Pounds in Two Weeks" ads that the cookies of my internet browser made sure filled my screen. Incidentally, these ads always popped up at the same moment I had cookie crumbs scattered on my shirt. I can't say I never take a gander at ads and articles like that anymore. The temptation to find an easy way out is ever-present. I know, though, that the quicker the weight falls off, the faster it comes back—and usually with a vengeance.

So I'm taking my time with loving my body and allowing consistency, not the scale, to be my gauge, because sometimes that scale acts like I purchased it from Hades and not Amazon. It will give me the same numbers week after week with no regard for how I've stepped up my nutrition or increased my time in the gym. "You're losing fat and gaining muscle. Don't pay attention to the scale" is what all the girls on TikTok say.

Even though I started my journey to see the scale change, I've stayed in the journey because I like what the process is birthing in me. (Those last few words felt like a book all by itself.) Recently I've started seeing movement on the scale again. Nothing too major—just a pound a week here or there. Sometimes I get discouraged because the decrease isn't as much as I wanted it to be.

When that happens, I remember to look at the full picture. Not just where I am but where I started. When I view it with the journey in mind, I see how the small decline is still getting me one step closer to my goal. Undervaluing the small wins robs us of the assurance and confidence that big wins are on the way.

I think about this as it relates to hope. It's not uncommon for us to miss the fulfillment of little hopes that maintain the faith we have for the big hopes that have not been answered. I was thinking about this the other day when I took my daughters to school. I was late getting out of the door, and their school recently changed the start time. I thought, *I hope I make it in time.* I pulled up with a minute or two to spare and hurried the girls out of the car. As soon as they were out, I was shifting my focus to the remaining tasks of the day when I felt hope tap me on the shoulder.

Undervaluing the small wins robs us of the assurance and confidence that big wins are on the way.

It was like hope wanted to remind me that it had shown up for me. I used the word casually but missed the comfort that accompanied the fulfillment of that hope. I took a pause and told God thank You for making my hope a reality.

God challenged me not to attempt to eliminate the usage of the word *hope* but rather to highlight how ever present it is in our lives and how frequently we ignore it. If you have ever hoped the recipe turns out good, the meeting is productive, your spouse makes it home safely, your child doesn't have homework, or you're able to get in bed as soon as possible, then you are well acquainted with the role that hope plays in getting you from that moment.

No wonder it requires so much momentum to build up the courage, faith, and trust connected to the big thing you're hoping for.

Remember Romans 15:13? "Now may the God of hope fill you with all joy and peace in believing, that you may abound in hope by the power of the Holy Spirit." The only way that we get to that place of abounding in hope is when we allow the Holy Spirit to reveal to us each and every moment when the God of hope consistently breathed on small moments. It reminds our soul when anxiety rises that hope is not just on the way; hope is here.

Couriers of Hope

What if I told you that even when you feel the most hopeless, you are surrounded by hope? It's hard to believe that this is possible when you find yourself overwhelmed by what you perceive as lack. It's hard to imagine that receiving hope in an area where you don't think you need it can help you in the place of your need.

I remember the first time I started experiencing knee pain when I was running. I was convinced I'd torn a ligament. One visit to a physical therapist helped me to learn that it wasn't my knee at all but rather my hip that was causing the pain. By working an area that wasn't in pain, it alleviated the place that felt the most tender.

A similar experience can be true when we are convinced we need God to move in one particular area. We are so focused on that one area that is causing us grief and stress that we miss how God is sustaining us in an unrelated place. My desire is to awaken you to the different sizes and shapes of divine hope that are available to us all.

Coming to a place where you're able to recognize that all the hope that is present may require you to reevaluate how you see the people you come across. Receiving hope is not always about the moments when someone we're connected to is able to serve our needs. Without a doubt that adds hope to our tank, but God knows how to use strangers to bring hope your way.

Before considering the ways that you can position yourself to receive hope, I want you to take some time to think about how you can give hope. Just a short exercise in practicing empathy can help you to become a courier of hope for someone else.

There are moments when you're out to eat at a busy time, and you can see the distress in the eyes of the restaurant team before they even head your way. It doesn't take deep contemplation to figure out that going out of your way to be kind and appreciative may be a glimmer of hope for them that day.

You can let someone new on your team know that they're doing a good job or even take the time to send a note of appreciation to a seemingly random person who has impacted your life. My daughter Makenzie is really good at this. She consistently takes the time to let me know that I'm doing a good job as a mother. Little does she know that being a good mom was something I was afraid I would not be able to do because of the age I got started. Each time she momentarily fills my cup, it doesn't just make me feel loved; it makes me feel hopeful that I'm doing a good job as a mother. I'm challenged to make sure that I maximize moments to do for others what she does for me.

Each day, we encounter people who are walking around with unique needs. We don't know, nor do we need to know, what those needs are. What we do know is that in the time that we share with them, we have an opportunity to be a glimpse of hope that they may not otherwise see. If the world has you, the world is never without hope.

One of the first scriptures God highlighted to me about hope was Colossians 1:27: "To them God willed to make known what are the riches of the glory of this mystery among the Gentiles: which is Christ in you, the hope of glory." The glory that people are hungry to experience inhabits the earth when you allow Christ in you to set the tone wherever you go.

I believe that at the core of our hope is the desire to feel like our lives have value and that we're progressing toward something better. As much, and as often, as we can offer someone that reassurance, we should. Lord knows there are moments when we all need it, so why not go out of our way to be it?

Take the time to look at the rhythm and responsibilities of the people in your world, and ask them, or God, how you can be an answer to their hope today. Do this only when you have capacity, and don't take no for an answer.

The girlfriend with the new baby needs a nap.

Your friend needs help folding laundry.

Your parents want to feel less alone as their lives change.

The world is in dire need of hope, and that means the world is in dire need of you.

If you're wondering what your purpose is and how you can make a difference with the cards you've been dealt, the answer is in the intentional hope that you spread. The manifestation of God's presence is experienced through the people who live their lives as couriers of hope. When your intentions are not to take or be seen, you are able to give and observe in a way that produces creative ways to help push someone further toward hope.

The world is

in dire need

of hope, and

that means the

world is in dire

need of you.

Interdependent Hope

Some of my friends like the idea of being able to serve someone else, but they bristle at the idea of being dependent on another person. Showing up for someone can be rewarding for you and the person receiving your gesture. It's not nearly as uncomfortable as the moments when our hope for the future requires the participation of another person.

If all we had to count on was ourselves and the Lord, maintaining hope would be easy. But for some reason, God has often wrapped up the fullness of our hope in another person. We become worried when we aren't sure whether a person has the wisdom, maturity, and sensitivity to partner with us in hanging on to hope.

A little hope goes a long way, but no hope goes no way. If you're partnered with someone who doesn't have the same hope as you do, then you can be sure that there will be tension. If you think by "partnership" I just mean romantic relationship, let me be clear: any person you're intentionally connected to is your partner in this thing called life.

Do you and your friends share the same hope? What about you and your faith leader? What about you and your coparent? One of the most important questions you should ask someone when getting to know them is, "What are your hopes?" When you share the same hope, you may not share the same philosophy or game plan, but you have an agreed-upon destination.

There will be moments when the success of your hope will require you to partner with another person. There is power in agreement and hopelessness in disunity. I'm praying that God would bring into your life people who share not only the same interests and hobbies but also the same hope. Breakthrough is birthed when there's a common goal and shared momentum to achieve it.

In the Bible, we see that God used two people with different circumstances to birth hope in a tough season. You know how our math teachers taught us how to work with positive and negative integers? Let's just say both of these individuals were in a negative position, but because they partnered in their vulnerability and hope, their negatives turned into a powerful positive.

I'm talking about Elijah and a nameless widow in 1 Kings 17. Elijah was one of the prophets in the Bible who received a lot of recognition for being what I would call "about that life!" This prophet did not mind doing the unexpected or saying what needed to be said, even if it put a target on his back. As valiant and determined as the prophet Elijah was, one of the most acclaimed moments in his life had nothing to do with taking down an enemy. It was a moment when he became a courier of hope for a widowed mother who was down to her last hope, and she became the same for him.

I'll provide you with some background. The region where Elijah and the widow resided was experiencing a drought. There seemed to be no end in sight, but Elijah stayed connected to God in the drought, and as a result God made sure he had constant provision. This widow had no idea that God was about to use her to be the source of Elijah's provision.

That was probably a good thing because had she known, she probably would have been dodging Elijah the way we dodge people when we owe them money. She only had enough provision left to make one last piece of bread for herself and her son before they faced the harsh reality of starving to death.

God destined for Elijah and this widow to become couriers of hope for one another, but it would not occur without vulnerability on both sides. They were both in need and could not allow themselves to be too prideful to admit it.

You need people, and needing people is not a sign of weakness. The acknowledgment of need is an opportunity to live authentically as who God has created you to be. In connection with others, we receive a hope that we cannot conjure on our own. Elijah and the widow possessed a shared hope of wanting to live, but neither had a clear path forward without the other.

You cannot force someone to share the same hopes as you do. That's a good thing, believe it or not. It's so much easier for you to choose your people with wisdom when you only have to worry about motivating them and not molding them.

You also have to be willing to open up and let someone into the place of your need. Elijah was a big-time prophet who was notorious for standing alone, but during this particular season of his life, he needed someone to help him. When you're the one used to giving hope to others, it's hard to admit when you're in need. Elijah demonstrated what happens when you learn to ask for what you need.

It may not have seemed like a big ask at any other time, but because they were in a drought, when Elijah asked the widow for some bread, he was asking for something big. Your ask seems big because of what's happening around you, but to someone who is in a different season, your ask may be small.

I'll give you an example. You may think that asking someone to read something you've written is taking too much of their time. On the other hand, there's someone who is waiting to hear your thoughts and would find pleasure in filling their time with something different. Or if you're a new mom and someone asks what they can do to help, then point out that laundry, show them the mop, and throw them the sponge. It may be a lot for you, but if they're in your life, give them the chance to help you become.

There are couriers of hope assigned to your destiny who can help you get out of a hopeless situation, but your vulnerability is the only way to unlock what they carry. They may not be able to help you in the area that you think matters the most, but they are able to help you keep a little hope alive until abundant hope finds its way to you.

Abundance Is Not Overflow

Though our older children are getting closer and closer to leaving home, as it stands we're a family of seven. When I plan for dinner,

I have learned to be very intentional about how much food I make. The goal is to make sure I have just enough food for everyone to eat, for the hungrier members to have second portions, and for a couple of people to have an option of leftovers for lunch the next day.

This is quite the science and one I've had to study over time, because I was making too much or too little food. On the nights when I did not have enough food, I would convince a few of the kids that ramen noodles were a gourmet option in comparison to what I'd whipped together. I'd receive some side-eye glances, but they went with the story anyway.

The nights when I made too much food were the worst. I could tell within a few days that the mountain of leftovers was going to go bad before we could plow through it. We'd make plates for unhoused individuals on some of the main streets in our neighborhood, or I'd give a ring to people I know who enjoy a good home-cooked meal.

On days when none of that worked, I'd feel the shame of throwing away perfectly good food. There are many things I'd like to have in excess, but if I had to choose between overflow and abundance, my choice would be abundance.

Abundance is not necessarily having more than you need. Abundance is knowing you'll never be in need. There's been a lot of conversation among mental and emotional wellness experts regarding an abundance mentality. That mentality is so powerful because it is not relegated to a moment but rather is a constant consciousness.

In one of David's psalms, he famously wrote, "The LORD is my shepherd; I shall not want" (Psalm 23:1). A word study of this famous scripture actually translates as "I have no lack." David mastered an abundance mentality that was directly related to his relationship with God. What a testament to his trust that his connection with God was all the resource he would ever need.

The widow in 1 Kings 17 must have learned this mentality firsthand. Can you imagine what it was like trusting God the first couple of days after Elijah relayed the Lord's promise to her that her bin of flour and jar of oil would not be used up?

On day one, she probably reached into the bin with relief and satisfaction that she no longer had to worry about anything. Day two rolled around, and because she was still walking out trust in this area of provision, she probably checked the bin and jar before she even hungered. I know I would have. As the days continued, she likely settled into the fact that God was really going to be faithful to provide enough flour and oil to make bread every single day and that she had nothing to worry about.

This book is coming to an end, but there's so much more life waiting for you outside of these pages. You're going to have moments when it feels like you're down to absolutely nothing, but God is going to send His provision in an unexpected way.

If you are intentional about acknowledging that God provided your need, not just once or twice but consistently, you'll understand that with God it's better to have abundance than it is to have overflow. Let's be honest—when we're having those inevitable moments of overflow, we are grateful to God, but our gratitude is different when God comes through in those moments when it seemed like all hope was lost.

As Paul wrote in Romans 15:13, I desire for you to "abound in hope." No matter how hopeless a season has been, you can trust that God's provision for your life includes an ever-present hope that awaits you each day. You'll know you are operating in abundance when you no longer reduce God to only moving in those big ways, but with humility and gratitude you acknowledge the little hopes throughout your life that have helped you to go a long way.

HUNGRY FOR HOPE

1. How can hope be contagious?

2. How does it feel to know that God has confidence in you? What does this confidence compel you to do?

3. How has someone in the past spread hope into your heart? What can you do for someone else today that could fill them with much-needed strength and hope?

CONCLUSION

There's nothing I love more than to share what I'm learning with the people God has allowed me to serve. As you can probably tell, I've spent a lot of time meditating on hope and the many ways it shows up in our lives. The journey has provided me with an anchor that I did not even know my soul needed.

As I was writing this book, there were many things that threatened to rob me of hope. Isn't it so on-brand for the Enemy to try to send you discouragement in the very area you're trying to serve someone else? We were in the middle of difficulty after difficulty, but for some reason I was not shaken.

My husband asked me one day, "How are you handling this with so much ease?" I told him I'm either close to having a mental breakdown and am delirious, or I have so much hope that everything is going to be okay that these setbacks don't scare me.

Now that we're somewhat on the other side of things, I'm pretty certain that it wasn't a mental breakdown. Instead, I think that sharing this message opened my eyes to the joy that comes with complete and utter trust that God's got my back. The doors were shutting and the window for opportunity was closing, but my heart was at peace.

I pray that I will always be able to maintain the hope in God's plan that I currently possess because it's been a light in trying times and a shield in a whirlwind of constant ups and downs. I directly attribute this season of unshakable faith to the revelation of hope that God has sent my way.

As the Woman Evolve ministry grows, we will host larger conferences than we ever have before. There's a version of me that would be shaking in my boots at the exponential growth. I feel sober, honored, and strategic about creating a safe space, but I don't feel over my head. I feel like I'm walking in God's hope for my life, and this walk has already taken into account the moments when I will need to stop and be refreshed.

I pray that at some point while you were reading this book, you got more than words and wisdom and received an anchor to help you in this crazy thing called life. Allow that word to become an anchor by meditating on it and countering negative thoughts with the assurance of God's faithfulness to deliver you.

Should you ever doubt this, you are not alone. Even Jesus wondered where God was in the midst of His suffering. But after Jesus expressed His pain, He did what we must all learn to do: Jesus surrendered His will to God's will (Matthew 26:39).

If you're going to be anchored to hope, there's just a couple of things I want you to know. There will be times when you find that you're adrift and more distant from God than you even realized.

The greatest gift you

can give yourself is

the reminder that if

you're still here, God's

still got a hope for

you in this earth.

You will see that you became anchored to the pursuit of success, the stress of your purpose, or the obligations of your world.

There's nothing wrong with you. This happens to the best of us. The greatest gift you can give yourself is the reminder that if you're still here, God's still got a hope for you in this earth. That is the only anchor worth holding on to, and that is the only anchor that will help you to maximize even your most challenging moments.

My friends have helped me during seasons when hope was obscure and fear was rampant. I pray that in the pages of this book I've done the same for you. Together we can share the breadcrumbs that help a generation never to feel lost again. As a community, we can rise up and become testimonies of what it means to lean into God's hope.

If we get this right, and I know that many of us will, the headlines won't scare us and the crises won't shake us. We'll recognize that new beginnings are buried in painful endings, and we'll refuse the insecurity and negativity that attempt to thwart us from our destiny. It won't be because we always feel strong and resilient, but because we have a divine expectation that even in our darkest hour there is still hope to be found.

NOTES

1. Allison Lau, "The Rise of Fad Diets," CNBC, January 11, 2021, https://www.cnbc.com/video/2021/01/11/how-dieting-became-a -71-billion-industry-from-atkins-and-paleo-to-noom.html.
2. Sarah Jakes, *Lost and Found: Finding Hope in the Detours of Life* (Minneapolis: Bethany House, 2015).
3. Touré Roberts, *Balance: Positioning Yourself to Do All Things Well* (Grand Rapids: Zondervan, 2022).
4. *Merriam-Webster*, s.v. "servant," accessed April 19, 2023, https://www.merriam-webster.com/dictionary/servant.
5. "What Is Hate Speech?," United Nations, https://www.un.org/en /hate-speech/understanding-hate-speech/what-is-hate-speech.
6. "What Is Hate Speech?"

ACKNOWLEDGMENTS

I really had no intention of writing a book this year. I was waiting to write a more extensive follow-up to my book *Woman Evolve*, but unpacking hope consumed my heart and mind. Collaborating with the Woman Evolve team each month for how we could continue to spread hope to the women connected to our movement inspired me to take all that I was learning and place it in this book. The contents of this book are an amalgamation of our content meetings, Hey You gatherings, random text messages, Slack communications, podcast conversations, and an embarrassing amount of memes.

The truth is that the team working behind the scenes to help this movement evolve are the real superheroes. Our amazing writers, graphic designers, social media strategists, producers, editors, team leads, and many more prove that it truly does take a village to raise a movement. (Or whatever the saying is lol.)

Many of the people who've poured their hearts into the movement have moved on to different phases of their lives; still, this ministry has been marked by their gifts and talents. Their unique perspectives offered me hope and support when my hope tank was running low.

Woman Evolve would not be the sisterhood it is without the delegation of women who've covered and prayed for me and our sisters. Their generosity knows no end. I am grateful for the many ways they pour into me with their words, hugs, DMs, and Chick-fil-A gift cards.

I could not be prouder of the gift God has given me in my publishing family. My incredible agents, Jan Miller and Shannon Marven, undoubtedly think more highly of my gist and voice than I do. I am grateful for your wisdom and vision for what's possible with the words God has placed on my heart. My friends at W Publishing have restored my hope in the publishing journey. I was wary that writing would lose its joy, but your patience with my creativity and sensitivity has allowed me to preserve my love for words while polishing my gift so that it can reach as many people as possible.

Lastly, because all that I do is anchored by their presence, is my incredible family. To my husband, whose very presence is a resurrected hope I'd long buried, you're the only person on the planet I want to be on a scavenger hunt for hope with. To my six heartbeats, now seven with Ty, that I call children: Who could have imagined that seeing you smile would be my favorite hobby? I love the sound of your laughter. I'll forever be cheering for you as you embark on your journey of hope. To my parents and siblings who believed in me when I was at my lowest: You were the life support that kept my hope in God alive. All that I do is your harvest too.

To me: Girl, I hope you never forget that you didn't hope for this. God hoped this for you. It started with Him; make sure it always ends with Him.

ABOUT THE AUTHOR

SARAH JAKES ROBERTS is a businesswoman, bestselling author, and media personality who expertly balances career, ministry, and family. She has been the driving force behind grassroots marketing for films, publications, and community programs that inspire and uplift people of all ages and backgrounds. Sarah is the daughter of Bishop T. D. Jakes and Mrs. Serita Jakes and pastors a dynamic community of artists and professionals alongside her husband, Touré. In 2017, Sarah launched Woman Evolve, a ministry that focuses on incubating every woman to her fullness. Since its conception, Woman Evolve has been successful at reaching and guiding thousands of women to awaken healing, wholeness, and love for themselves and others. Sarah is most proud of the life she and her husband have built together. Together they have six beautiful children and split their time between Los Angeles, California, and Denver, Colorado.